STUDIES IN ECONOMIC AND SOCIAL HISTORY

Th... ...conomic History Soc... ...ations of the key ...ei... ...tory in which advances have ...ently been made or in which there has been significant debate.

Originally entitled 'Studies in Economic History', in 1974 the series had its scope extended to include topics in social history, and the new series title, 'Studies in Economic and Social History', signalises this development.

The series gives readers access to the best work done, helps them to draw their own conclusions in major fields of study, and by means of the critical bibliography in each book guides them in the selection of further reading. The aim is to provide a springboard to further work rather than a set of pre-packaged conclusions or short-cuts.

ECONOMIC HISTORY SOCIETY

The Economic History Society, which numbers around 3000 members, publishes the *Economic History Review* four times a year (free to members) and holds an annual conference. Enquiries about membership should be addressed to the Assistant Secretary, Economic History Society, PO Box 190, 1 Greville Road, Cambridge CB1 3QG. Full-time students may join at special rates.

STUDIES IN ECONOMIC AND SOCIAL HISTORY

Edited for the Economic History Society by L. A. Clarkson

PUBLISHED

Bill Albert Latin America and the World Economy from Independence to 1930
B. W. E. Alford Depression and Recovery? British Economic Growth, 1918–1939
B. W. E. Alford British Economic Performance, 1945–1975
Michael Anderson Approaches to the History of the Western Family, 1500–1914
Michael Anderson Population Change in North-Western Europe, 1750–1850

Published titles continued overleaf

P. J. Cain Economic Foundations of British Overseas Expansion, 1815–1914
S. D. Chapman The Cotton Industry in the Industrial Revolution 2nd edition
Neil Charlesworth British Rule and the Indian Economy, 1800–1914
J. A. Chartres Internal Trade in England, 1500–1700
R. A. Church The Great Victorian Boom, 1850–1873
L. A. Clarkson Proto-Industrialization: The First Phase of Industrialization?
D. C. Coleman Industry in Tudor and Stuart England
Michael Collins Banks and Industrial Finance in Britain, 1800–1939
P. L. Cottrell British Overseas Investment in the Nineteenth Century
M. A. Crowther Social Policy in Britain 1914–1939
Ralph Davis English Overseas Trade, 1500–1700
Ian Drummond The Gold Standard
Alan Dyer Decline and Growth in English Towns, 1400–1640
M. E. Falkus The Industrialisation of Russia, 1700–1914
Peter Fearon The Origins and Nature of the Great Slump, 1929–1932
T. R. Gourvish Railways and the British Economy, 1830–1914
Robert Gray The Aristocracy of Labour in Nineteenth-century Britain, c. 1850–1900
J. R. Harris The British Iron Industry, 1700–1850
John Hatcher Plague, Population and the English Economy, 1348–1530
J. R. Hay The Origins of the Liberal Welfare Reforms, 1906–1914
R. H. Hilton The Decline of Serfdom in Medieval England
E. L. Jones The Development of English Agriculture, 1815–1973
John Lovell British Trade Unions, 1875–1933
Donald N. McCloskey Econometric History
Hugh McLeod Religion and the Working Class in Nineteenth-Century Britain
W. J. Macpherson The Economic Development of Japan c. 1868–1941
J. D. Marshall The Old Poor Law, 1795–1834
Alan S. Milward The Economic Effects of the Two World Wars on Britain
G. E. Mingay Enclosure and the Small Farmer in the Age of the Industrial Revolution
Rosalind Mitchison British Population Change since 1860
R. J. Morris Class and Class Consciousness in the Industrial Revolution, 1780–1850
J. Forbes Munro Britain in Tropical Africa, 1880–1960
A. E. Musson British Trade Unions, 1800–1875
Patrick K. O'Brien The Economic Effects of the American Civil War
Cormac Ó Gráda The Great Irish Famine
R. B. Outhwaite Inflation in Tudor and Early Stuart England
R. J. Overy The Nazi Economic Recovery, 1932–1938
P. L. Payne British Entrepreneurship in the Nineteenth Century 2nd edition
G. C. Peden Keynes, The Treasury and British Economic Policy
Roy Porter Disease, Medicine and Society in England, 1550–1860
G. D. Ramsay The English Woollen Industry, 1500–1750
Elizabeth Roberts Women's Work 1840–1940
Richard Rodger Housing in Urban Britain 1780–1914
Michael E. Rose The Relief of Poverty, 1834–1914
Michael Sanderson Education, Economic Change and Society in England, 1780–1870
S. B. Saul The Myth of the Great Depression, 1873–1896
Paul Slack The English Poor Law 1531–1782
Arthur J. Taylor Laissez-faire and State Intervention in Nineteenth-century Britain
Peter Temin Causal Factors in American Economic Growth in the Nineteenth Century
Joan Thirsk England's Agricultural Regions and Agrarian History, 1500–1750
Michael Turner Enclosures in Britain, 1750–1830
Margaret Walsh The American Frontier Revisited
J. R. Ward Poverty and Progress in the Caribbean 1800–1960

OTHER TITLES IN PREPARATION

Decline and Growth in English Towns, 1400–1640

Prepared for
the Economic History Society by

ALAN DYER
University of Wales

MACMILLAN

First published in 1991

Published by
MACMILLAN EDUCATION LTD
Houndmills, Basingstoke, Hampshire RG21 2XS
and London
Companies and representatives
throughout the world

Printed in Hong Kong

British Library Cataloguing in Publication Data
Dyer, Alan 1941–
Decline and growth in English towns, 1400–1640. — (Studies
in economic and social history).
1. England. Towns, history
I. Title II. Economic History Society III. Series
942.009732
ISBN 0–333–42069–1

Series Standing Order

If you would like to receive future titles in this series as they are
published, you can make use of our standing order facility. To place a
standing order please contact your bookseller or, in case of difficulty,
write to us at the address below with your name and address and the
name of the series. Please state with which title you wish to begin your
standing order. (If you live outside the United Kingdom we may not
have the rights for your area, in which case we will forward your order
to the publisher concerned.)

Customer Services Department, Macmillan Distribution Ltd
Houndmills, Basingstoke, Hampshire, RG21 2XS, England.

Contents

	List of Maps	6
	Note on References	6
	Editor's Preface	7
	Acknowledgement	8
1	Introduction	9
2	The Background to the Controversy	12
3	Urban Fortunes Before 1450	20
4	Urban Crisis at the End of the Middle Ages	25
5	The Problems of Evidence	37
6	Expansion and Decline 1540–1640	51
7	Conclusion	58
	Appendices	64
	Select Bibliography	75
	Index	83

List of Maps

1 English counties, showing changes in wealth   22

2 English counties, showing changes in taxpaying   41
population

3 England and Wales, showing towns mentioned in the   62–3
text

Note on References

References in the text within square brackets relate to the numbered items in the Bibliography; where page numbers are given, they are printed in italics, for example [76, *231*].

Editor's Preface

When this series was established in 1968 the first editor, the late Professor M. W. Flinn, laid down three guiding principles. The books should be concerned with important fields of economic history; they should be surveys of the current state of scholarship rather than a vehicle for the specialist views of the authors, and above all, they were to be introductions to their subject and not 'a set of pre-packaged conclusions'. These aims were admirably fulfilled by Professor Flinn and by his successor, Professor T. C. Smout, who took over the series in 1977. As it passes to its third editor and approaches its third decade, the principles remain the same.

Nevertheless, times change, even though principles do not. The series was launched when the study of economic history was burgeoning and new findings and fresh interpretations were threatening to overwhelm students – and sometimes their teachers. The series has expanded its scope, particularly in the area of social history – although the distinction between 'economic' and 'social' is sometimes hard to recognize and even more difficult to sustain. It has also extended geographically; its roots remain firmly British, but an increasing number of titles is concerned with the economic and social history of the wider world. However, some of the early titles can no longer claim to be introductions to the current state of scholarship; and the discipline as a whole lacks the heady growth of the 1960s and early 1970s. To overcome the first problem a number of new editions, or entirely new works, have been commissioned – some have already appeared. To deal with the second, the aim remains to publish up-to-date introductions to important areas of debate. If the series can demonstrate to students and their teachers the importance of the discipline of economic and social history and excite its further study, it will continue the task so ably begun by its first two editors.

The Queen's University of Belfast

L. A. CLARKSON
General Editor

7

Acknowledgement

The jacket illustration shows a detail from Jacobus Millerd's map of Bristol, 1673. Every effort has been made to trace the copyright-holder for this map, and if the copyright-holder has been inadvertently overlooked the publishers will be pleased to make the necessary arrangement at the first opportunity.

1 Introduction

Most of those [cities] which were great once are small today;
and those which in my own lifetime have grown to greatness,
were small enough in the old days.

(Herodotus, *c.* 435 BC)

What was the condition of English towns between the fourteenth
and the sixteenth centuries? Were their populations growing or
contracting, were their economies depressed, prospering or
merely coping with the stresses of the age? One would have
thought that after many years of historical enquiry we should
have answered these questions. But the problem of urban decline
has grown into a fully blown Historical Controversy, with battle
lines drawn, the protagonists ranged behind the banners of
pessimism and optimism, and the outline of the contested terrain
obscured by heat and smoke. As with most historical debates, the
result is that research is stimulated, a few questions are answered
(at the cost of the creation of some new ones) and we are left
with only the certainty that all simple answers must be wrong.

There are two main reasons why no consensus has emerged on
this topic. The first lies in the definition of terms – there is as yet
no agreement on what words like 'town', 'decay', 'prosperity' or
'vigour' actually mean in this context. Add to this the second
problem, which is the failure as yet to establish basic facts and
interpretations, such as how population was changing or whether
the nation as a whole was getting wealthier or poorer, and the
magnitude of the task becomes clearer.

Towns are important. Perhaps this is itself enough to justify
the study of this topic, but if more is needed, then we could
point to the fact that urban history supplies a cross-section
through much of the history of any period with which it is
concerned. One cannot understand what happens to the towns at
the end of the middle ages without appreciating what was

9

occurring in the countryside, on the continent, in the politics of parliament and monarchy, and much else. These are all issues which will appear as our theme unfolds. The topic is also a good illustration of the essence of the historian's craft, for how do we handle the unreliable evidence which is all we have to reconstruct past reality? How in particular do we come to a balanced view, when we have to weigh on the one hand a mass of positive written statements against, on the other, the material which has been lost, or was never written because no one saw any point in recording it? These latter aspects we must reconstruct in our imagination if we are to consider both sides of the question with impartiality. The relevance of these considerations will emerge below.

To return to problems of definition. Throughout the pages which follow the reader should bear in mind the need to specify what sorts of decline are under discussion. Decline may be relative – that is to say towns may lose either wealth or people by comparison with the countryside, or other towns. For instance, they could grow in wealth but still 'decline' in their share of national wealth if the countryside was becoming richer faster. Decline may also be absolute, that is the level it reaches at any one time is less than it had been in the immediate past – but this raises the problem of time scales, for what is to be taken as the benchmark against which later change is to be measured? Coventry grew in wealth and size between about 1370 and 1430, and then fell back. Compared with its state in 1430 it had clearly declined by 1640, but if we were to compare it with its condition in 1370, before its temporary boom, then our conclusion would be different. Is the boom or the slump the striking phenomenon which needs to be noticed and explained?

The two aspects of urban achievement which we can measure, wealth and population, both present problems. In the pre-industrial economy, when towns attracted large numbers of very poor people, a reduced population was not necessarily a bad thing, for the slimmed town might well enjoy full employment and an enhanced per capita income. Increasing population may well have led to more unemployment, poverty and slum housing, as seems often to have happened by the early seventeenth century. Similarly, the concept of wealth is a slippery one; do we

10

mean per capita wealth, which could be increased just by killing off some of the population (especially the poor), or the wealth of the small group of businessmen who ruled most towns and paid most of the taxes, or the total riches of the community as a whole?

2 The Background to the Controversy

The concept of urban decline in our period has a very long ancestry behind it. It was claimed to exist in the period itself and the modern view of the later middle ages as a period dominated by depression and decay has been very influential. Yet a century ago, in 1894, Mrs Green's *Town Life in the Fifteenth Century* could innocently speak of a 'prosperous maturity' in the boroughs she studied. As Lipson's monumental *Economic History of England* was published (from 1915 onwards) the broad outline of the traditional view of decline was becoming clear. The complaints of the big towns in trouble, preserved in the archives of parliament and crown – Lincoln, Great Yarmouth, Winchester, York and Oxford for instance – are conspicuous, though the evidence of prosperity is not ignored. Many of these problems are put down to the loss of the cloth industry to the countryside, though there is no attempt to suggest that all towns are decayed. During the 1940s and 50s it became established that falling population caused by plague should be the basis of interpreting most aspects of English economic history after 1350 and this encouraged belief in the idea of a general decline of towns.

Two developments instigated the debate over urban decline which has simmered ever since. The first was the development of the concept of *urban* history, the idea that towns formed in themselves a worthy and coherent theme for historians. The result was a spate of studies of individual towns, and a demand for a general theory of urban development in this country, into which the history of individual towns might be fitted. The second, of particular relevance to our topic, was the publication in 1962 of Bridbury's *Economic Growth . . .* [28] which in uncompromising and effective style promulgated a strikingly unconventional view of a prosperous late middle ages in which the towns were rich and vigorous. Reactions followed, most of them hostile and attempting to restore an orthodoxy of predomi-

12

nant decline, conspicuous among them R. B. Dobson's article in 1977 [29]. In 1979, the high-water mark of the decline school, came the publication of Phythian-Adams' *Desolation of a City* [76] which through a study of Coventry in crisis expounds the case for general decline at its most extreme, with language and attitudes as uncompromising as those of Bridbury for the other faction. The work of Phythian-Adams was particularly important in extending the concept of a late medieval urban crisis into the sixteenth century, with a climax as late as the period 1520–60 [30].

Meanwhile towns in the sixteenth and seventeenth centuries were given a pioneering general synthesis by Clark and Slack's *Crisis and Order* published in 1972 [19], reinforced by *English Towns in Transition* (1976) [20]. Their view stresses the dominating presence of continuing problems of poverty, plague and economic inadequacy right up to the later seventeenth century, thus extending the chronology of urban difficulty. Since then the opposing camps have continued to snipe at each other without any great measure of agreement, with further ammunition provided by the appearance of some very useful detailed studies of individual towns such as Winchester and Colchester. During the 1980s there does seem to have been a narrowing of the divide, with no side appearing to be getting the better of the argument and the most recent attempt at a summary stressing the ambiguity of the evidence and the importance of the general restructuring of the late medieval economy [36].

Before we can consider the experience of individual towns between 1300 and 1550 it is essential that the economic and social background is understood, for much hangs upon it [1–6]. The single most important trend was a dramatic loss of population. In 1300 the English population may have stood at 4–6 million; repeated epidemics of bubonic plague from 1349 onwards brought the total down to 2.75–3.0 million by 1377 [15]. Although this represented a great reduction on the 1300 level, it probably reflected a measure of recovery from the first effects of the plague, for towns could still find a reserve of potential migrants in the countryside, and there appeared in 1377 to be few symptoms of real damage from population shortage. Thus a recent estimate of Norwich's population suggests that a total of 25,000 in 1333 fell to about 7500 by 1377 [17]; yet such

13

reductions, which look catastrophic to modern eyes, seem to have been accommodated with minimal disruption. By the 1360s or 70s a relatively ideal balance between urban population and resources had been created. But plague epidemics continued, and by the early fifteenth century it appears that population was continuing to drift downwards, with signs that shortage of people was becoming a real problem. The bottom of the trough may have been reached by mid-century, and from the 1470s onwards some historians see signs of a slow recovery, though others find no trace of any upswing until the sixteenth century, with epidemics continuing to cut back any incipient improvement. Those who have tried to construct a general view of the late medieval economy (a hazardous task with minimal statistical data) have tended to see it as running parallel to the developments in population described above, with a period of prosperity from about 1370 which dwindled away after 1420 into pronounced depression in the 1450s; recovery in many areas is noted from the 1470s onwards.

If we look at the major aspects of the economy in more detail, food prices show a marked fall from about 1380 onwards, presumably as plague mortality eventually reduced demand, with the lowest point of the depression reached between 1440 and 1460; then there was a slight recovery, followed after 1510 by the beginnings of the great Tudor inflation. Wages increased rapidly almost immediately after the first plague and continued to rise due to a shortage of labour, so that the combined effect of falling food prices and rising wages improved the standard of living of the wage-earner very substantially. His prosperity peaked between about 1415 and 1510 – in some crafts the buying power of wages doubled between the 1340s and 1480s. However, such wage-earners were in a minority and few people in the countryside would have had access to wages outside the harvest period; anyone primarily dependent on selling food in the marketplace would have not enjoyed such affluence.

Agriculture was the dominant sector of the economy and it was the countryside which determined the prosperity of the nation as a whole. Here the depressed level of agricultural prices was crucial. Great estates gave up unrewarding direct exploitat-ation and rented out their lands. Peasant farming was transformed by the increased availability of land so that the numbers of the

14

landless and of very small holdings fell, and the better-off peasant farmers, soon to be termed the Tudor yeomen, began to emerge. Rural populations fell strikingly. In most regions corn growing gave way to pastoral agriculture, but local and regional conditions varied enormously [66–69]. In the south-east, where clothmaking and London stimulated the market demand for foodstuffs, farming did relatively well; the south-west, where the cloth industry was growing fast, saw prosperity for localities which could sell food to the weavers; in the midlands farmers were forced to turn from corn to sheep and cattle; but in the north of England there seems little sign of rural prosperity. It is very difficult to produce a general balance sheet from this, with some areas prosperous and others depressed, and it is even more difficult to predict the impact of it all on the spending patterns of the different rural social groups.

The cloth industry was an unqualified bright spot to contrast with the chequered agrarian picture [4]. English cloth captured an increasing share of European markets from the mid-fourteenth century right up to the check it suffered in the 1550s. In 1360, about 8000 standard-sized cloths were being exported; this total grew to about 57,000 by around 1440 and after a mid-century setback, approached 80,000 in 1500 and nearly 120,000 by 1540 [59]. When the unknown, but probably increasing, domestic consumption is added to these totals we have a picture of remarkable growth, achieved against considerable difficulties in continental markets. The textile industry generated much more employment than any other contemporary craft and stimulated the agricultural sector too: transport and shipping services were also involved, and large accumulations of merchant capital built up. A complementary movement to the rise of the cloth trade was supplied by declining shipments of raw wool, once England's great source of export earnings. As more wool was required for the expanding domestic woollen manufactures, wool exports fell from a peak of about 35,000 sacks per year around 1360 to less than 10,000 after 1420 and a modest 5000 or fewer by the 1520s [59]. These two trends caused major shifts in the regional pattern of wealth, for the wool trade had enriched the north-east, while the textile industry lay mostly in the south-east and south-west.

The other topic which we must cover is foreign trade in general [58–65]. The shift from wool to cloth as England's

15

dominant export had a drastic effect on the fortunes of most of the country's ports, with the east coast deeply damaged and some of the ports of the south-east and south-west growing in significance. Trade is a two-way affair, and imports tended to mirror the pattern of exports. The greatest growth of all was enjoyed by London, which absorbed an increasing proportion of cloth exports and the reciprocal imports of manufactured and luxury goods: nearly all the provincial ports were undermined by this trend, which gave the capital something approaching a monopoly by the early sixteenth century when three-quarters or more of the total exports of English cloth passed down the Thames.

One last point remains of this general survey: how do all these developments interact to determine changes in the standard of living of the different groups in English society [6]? We have already noted how economic trends could harm some regions, with areas like the north-east hit hard by changes in both agriculture and trade and industry: Lincolnshire and the East Riding of Yorkshire, for instance, lost their profitable wool producing and shipping activities while their corn growing areas suffered from their distance from expanding markets. London and the south-east, in contrast, benefited from changes in industry and trade, which in turn provided markets for food producers in the countryside. This geographical dimension must be fitted beside social changes in the countryside. On the optimistic side, wages rose and land holdings expanded, soil fertility improved and part-time work in the cloth industry became available while rent payments in cash absorbed less of household income at all levels. Yet the fall in food prices meant that the peasant farmer received less for his food while he had to pay more in wages to his hired labour. Where market demand was unpromising, many peasants must have fallen back on subsistence farming which supplied their household needs without buying in very much from the outside world. There is evidence of improving living standards in the countryside, as shown by better housing and diet, but apart from clothing, there is little sign in peasant households of purchases of the sort of goods which towns would have supplied. Evidently, while there were very considerable improvements in the security and freedom of those peasants who survived the epidemics, these advantages

16

were not necessarily accompanied by particularly large increases in the money they had to spend in town shops [6].

Much of the above material has been aimed at providing a basis for assessing a most vital question for the purposes of our enquiry into urban decline – how might all these trends affect urban prosperity? Townsmen benefited from the distribution of the capital, homes, land and employment of the plague dead amongst the reduced numbers of the survivors. But as repeated epidemics further eroded the population, wages rose and rural incomes lost their buoyancy, so that by about 1420, towns found themselves in a more difficult position. We have seen above that glib assumptions once made about the existence of a rural prosperity which could be exploited by urban businesses can no longer be sustained.

Probably the most serious consequence lay in a shortage of labour. At many periods in the past towns were reliant on a stream of migrants from the countryside to maintain their populations, for towns were intrinsically unhealthy places and were especially prone to bubonic plague, the dominant disease of the period. If deprived of this regular transfusion of people, most towns would have contracted. Towns with falling populations were not necessarily being impoverished, for the survivors could share a stable or gently shrinking cake amongst a number of inhabitants which was reducing rather more quickly, thus maintaining per capita incomes. But there came a point when town businesses could not find an adequate supply of labour to replace the epidemic losses of a fifteenth century during which plague and other diseases struck hard and often [13;14]. As long as the countryside produced more people than it could employ, towns could attract the migrants they needed, but in the fifteenth century there was land and employment available aplenty in rural areas. Probably high wages alone could have tempted the migrants in, but this added to already high labour costs and made urban industries uneconomic in competition with cheaper products made in the English countryside or abroad. There are indications of labour shortage throughout the period 1370–1560. In 1381 we find a shortage of male tradesmen allowing women in prosperous towns such as York to work independently at traditionally masculine crafts like those of smith or carpenter [12]. Thus while there were many features of late medieval

17

economic change which should have stimulated town businesses, such as increasing cloth exports and rising living standards in both town and country, the consequences of falling population also presented a serious challenge to the urban economy.

Towns had always been first and foremost market centres before some assumed an industrial role, and most small towns earned their living by their weekly markets which brought in country custom to their shops. The economic trends of the period would have had a mixed impact on the market town. Did the better wages earned by the landless make much difference? What market remained for foodstuffs was of great importance to farmers. Yet if small-scale subsistence farming also increased, this would involve a big reduction in the use of markets. Certainly the decline of large-scale demesne farming reduced the disposal of large accumulations of foodstuffs, although great households would now be more reliant on local markets for their supplies.

The most striking discovery made by the historians of late medieval marketing is an apparently dramatic collapse in the number of markets scattered over the face of the English provinces. A recent study [56] of 21 counties shows that by 1349 as many as 1003 places either were recorded as possessing a market or (much more commonly) had a royal charter conferring the right to hold a market lodged in the archives of the crown. But of these many places, only some 372 – a mere 37 per cent – retained their markets in the sixteenth century. This implies a massive reduction in the numbers of small market towns and so a fresh dimension to the concept of urban decline; indeed it has been described as 'a massive de-urbanisation' and 'a discontinuity in the English urban system exceeded in its severity only by the collapse of urban civilization at the end of the Roman occupation' [57]. This sounds serious.

Yet on closer examination, some flaws appear in this argument. Most of our evidence of the existence of these markets is derived from the grant of a royal charter, without any other record to show whether the projected market was ever actually founded, or how long it lasted. The sites of some of these grants lie very close to one another, as if they represent successive attempts to exploit the same gap in the market network, with the failure of one attempt leading to another in a nearby village and so on. The evidence covers two centuries or more and there is no clue as to

18

what was the total in operation at any one time. More seriously, for it must be true that many of these foundations did operate for some time at least, it may be questioned whether such villages-with-markets ever reached the point where we could call them towns. They seem to have been primarily concerned with supplying food in small quantities to landless peasants too poor to travel to a market more than a couple of miles from their homes [56]. This sort of demand cannot have supported the range of businesses which we would expect in a fully fledged market town. The eradication of competition from these tiny rural markets may well have actually strengthened the survivors, still amounting to a remarkable national total of over 600 in the sixteenth century. Some confirmation of this possibility is provided by the fact that the bigger market towns seem rather larger in the 1520s than they had been in the 1370s. Thus this rather alarming evidence of apparently disastrous decline can be made to reflect a strengthening of the true market town.

3 Urban Fortunes Before 1450

One of the salient features of the early and high middle ages was a great wave of urbanisation involving an expansion of the size and numbers of towns and the establishment of many new towns. It is not until this process ran out of steam in around 1300, along with the levelling out of economic and demographic growth, that the issue of urban decline is likely to be relevant. Urban problems at this point were chiefly connected with the cloth industry [8]. The manufacture was then concentrated in Newcastle, York, Beverley, Lincoln, Stamford, Leicester, Northampton, Oxford and Winchester, and from most of these towns came complaints of difficulty before or about 1300. The cause is not clear, for neither foreign competition nor migration to rural areas appears to have been a major factor. It may well be that things were not as black as they were painted; but it certainly seems true that Stamford, Oxford, Leicester and Northampton had lost their old industrial importance by the early 1300s. In other towns, most prominently York and Lincoln, a recovery was staged in the fourteenth century, most clearly in the case of York, which had grown to become the largest provincial city by 1377.

The later fourteenth century urban scene was shaped in part by two linked trends – the declining volume of wool exports and the remarkable increase in cloth exports to the continent. As the trade in wool ran down, the towns which had gathered and shipped it were thrown into decline. These places often coincided with the towns in the east midlands and north-east England which had already been hit by the migration of the old cloth manufacture, Lincoln, Stamford and Northampton; the east coast ports such as Boston and Lynn, once major centres of foreign trade, lost much of their commerce. Late fourteenth century cloth production was centred in Somerset and Wiltshire and in a region stretching eastwards from Hampshire to Kent, Hertfordshire and Essex. In the fifteenth century it spread into Suffolk in the east

20

and Devon in the west. This locational pattern shifted the industrial centre of gravity to the south and, along with the growth of London, left the towns of the north and north-east on the periphery. Although much of this development went on in the countryside, rural industry often stimulated urban growth by turning villages into small towns and creating new roles for existing towns as marketing, supply and finishing centres for the country weavers. Much was once made of the influence of the fulling mill, which mechanised the process of cloth finishing and needed fast-flowing streams for its power, usually found far from towns. But its importance has been exaggerated, as illustrated by cities such as Salisbury and Worcester which managed to run flourishing urban industries in lowland river valleys.

Thus the towns which appear to have been in decline were concentrated in the regions most affected by these changes. Beverley and the east midlands centres of Nottingham, Leicester, Lincoln, Stamford and Newark were most prominent here, though the impoverishing of their rural regions in the agricultural restructuring of the period may well have been a contributory factor. The seven counties of Derby, Nottingham, Rutland, Bedford, Cambridge, Norfolk, and Lincoln are all among the bottom ten when growth in taxable wealth between 1334 and 1524 is calculated, and Lincolnshire, one of the wealthiest and most densely populated areas in the whole country in 1300, was reduced to the twenty-fifth richest shire in 1525 [68;69; see Map 1]. These changes reflected sweeping transformations in the nature of the rural economy and the population it could support, so that one Lincolnshire rector in 1437 could explain the depopulation of his village in terms of 'lack of parishioners, the fewness of peasants, their low wages, the bareness of the lands, the lack of cultivation, pestilences and epidemics with which the Lord afflicts His people' [68, 180].

Many of the towns listed were linked in a common trading system, operating through the ports of Hull, Boston and Lynn. Here we are dealing with a whole depressed region, a problem in which town and country were both inextricably involved and which is not helpfully considered in terms of urban decline alone. Often the downward path of these places was a long one, so that pleas of poverty were still being made in the early sixteenth century. Within this single region there were separate factors

21

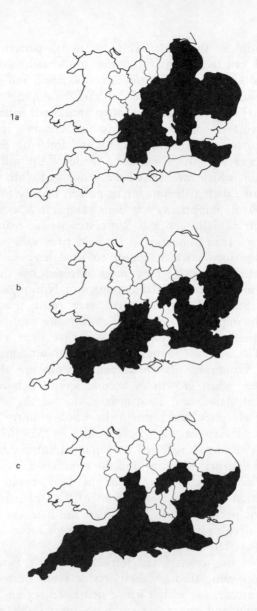

Map 1 *Changes in taxable wealth in 32 English counties 1334–1524/5.*
■ = *Upper half; a = 1334; b = 1524/5; c = growth 1334–1524/5.*
Major towns excluded. Calculated as £s/sq. mile.

22

connected with the problems of the fishing industry. Scarborough in the early fifteenth century was a leading fishing port but its fleet dwindled [92]. Great Yarmouth was a conspicuous casualty, its fishing fleet failing to compete with other east coast towns and especially with the Netherlanders, whose methods were more efficient [81]. Its merchant fleet was damaged by war, piracy and the general east coast complaint of a silting harbour, a daunting problem in an age without effective dredgers. The whole coastline was sinking, which slowed rivers and thus encouraged silting. Yarmouth's difficulties, beginning as early as 1350 and stabilised by the early 1400s, pre-date the classic period of urban decay and seem particular to itself.

In the case of Boston [41] we have one of the richest towns of 1334, ranked at fourth, which had sunk to twenty-second in wealth by the 1520s. As a major wool shipping port, accounting for at least a third of the national total around 1300, Boston was inevitably hit hard as English wool exports fell, coupled with the migration of its colony of foreign merchants to London and elsewhere. But Boston seems quite prosperous in its shrunken state in the early sixteenth century, which suggests that the halving of its population had left the survivors with per capita wealth which was not too badly depleted.

Lincoln [82] was a prominent participant in the drama of urban decline, taking a remarkably long period to go downhill, which leads one to suspect either that some of its complaints were exaggerated, or that there were unsung minor recoveries to set against the problem periods. Despite much fuss about its failing cloth industry, it was still the seventh wealthiest city in 1334 and the fifth largest in 1377. The city still ranked tenth in size in 1524 though its wealth had shrunk to twentieth. With Lynn, Boston and Beverley, this makes Lincoln one of the most conspicuous casualties of the period, for unlike many of the other large towns in trouble, the members of this quartet never recovered their previous status, though they remained important market towns in their own localities. Lincoln's trade depended on water routes to the Trent (silted by 1335) and to the sea at Boston (deteriorating by 1500); the effect would have been serious even had the local wool trade and cloth industry not been failing. Pleas of poverty from before 1300 were renewed throughout the fifteenth century and Lincoln appeared more often than any other city in the

23

manoeuvres which led to reduced tax burdens and other concessions from the central government, perhaps making its decline more conspicuous than it deserves to be.

Winchester [98] is a good parallel to Lincoln, for its decline was even more drawn out. A rival to London as capital and of great importance before 1200, it was damaged by London's victory, by the creation of a local rival in the foundation of the new town of Salisbury, and by the loss of its international fair. Complaints of decay began in 1204 and were repeated intermittently until the Tudor period. In fact there was a revival, based on a cloth industry, which enjoyed a brief boom until about 1410 and then ran down; population rose from something over 4000 in 1377 to over 7000 in 1417 before dropping again to about 4000 in the 1520s; its wealth fell from twelfth in 1334 to thirty-fifth in 1524/5. As in York, a migrating textile industry did much of the later damage, but there was no sign of a revival in the sixteenth century such as occurred in York. Winchester went downhill in stages over more than three centuries, with periods of remission and even of perverse growth occupying more time than did the years of actual deterioration; consequently the reasons for its decline were especially numerous and localised.

24

4 Urban Crisis at the End of the Middle Ages

With the middle years of the fifteenth century we enter the classic period of alleged urban decay. The years around 1450 were marked by widespread economic difficulty [3]. Foreign trade was hit hard by the loss of Normandy and Gascony as the Hundred Years War slid to its disastrous conclusion. Anglo–French trade in general recovered only slowly after the peace of 1453, and even before this date English merchants had lost their access to the Baltic region. External trade slumped, with cloth exports, averaging about 57,000 cloths in the early 1440s, dropping to about 30,000 in the early 1460s. Recovery came in the 1470s, the last two decades of the century showing a marked upswing, but the mid-century depression, while it lasted, must have presented a severe challenge to the commercial prosperity of many English towns.

The slump coincided with domestic political instability. The Wars of the Roses stretched from 1455 to 1487, with a peak of violence in 1460–1, but over these 32 years, actual fighting occupied a mere 12 or 13 weeks. In 1461 the Lancastrian army on its march to London was alleged to have sacked towns along the road from Lincolnshire but there is little supporting evidence for this story. Disorder in Wales and its borders may have been more serious and protracted. Insecurity is always bad for trade, but there is little in the written record which supports suggestions of serious damage. At least the weakness of the central government led to a relatively light tax burden and an avoidance of foreign wars on which that money would have been spent.

These were also years in which bubonic plague seems to have become centred on the towns, with less effect on the countryside, and although we know little about the impact of these epidemics they must have contributed largely to the difficulty most towns seem to have experienced in keeping up their populations when migrants were in short supply [12–16]. Deaths in leading

25

merchant families led to the disappearance of major businesses and the dispersion of accumulations of capital. Towards the end of the fifteenth century there began a serious threat to the prosperity of the provincial ports in the apparently irresistible competition of London. The customs records show that by about 1400 London had grasped around 50 per cent of cloth exports, but made no further headway until about 1480 when its share rose to around 70 per cent, over 80 per cent by the 1530s and nearly 90 per cent by mid century [59]. The volume of exports was rising fast, and therefore not all provincial ports were left with fewer cloths on their quays, but in many places the effect was very depressing. The earliest and hardest hit victims were the east coast ports from Hull down to Great Yarmouth, including Boston and Lynn. Wine imports tell an even sorrier tale, with Boston and Lynn's trade almost vanished. Along the south coast and in the south-west the effect of London's magnetism took longer to make its mark, with Exeter and Southampton keeping up a respectable showing in cloth exports into the early years of the sixteenth century. When it came, Bristol's eclipse was remarkably rapid, for it reached an export peak of 8614 cloths in 1495–6 but fell away rapidly to a very bad year in 1505–6 with only 2735. Prominent Bristol merchants migrated to London, taking with them their capital and trading contacts. Since those who exported cloth usually imported foreign luxuries in return, these profitable trades were also lost to London.

The attraction of the capital seems to have been twofold. London was the obvious gateway to Antwerp, on which most of England's foreign trade had become riveted. And London's banking, credit and exchange facilities were much better than those of any other port. But other towns still made money from cloth as it was processed, sold, packed and transported to the capital, and we know little of the domestic coastal trade of the provincial ports because the records are lost. The expansion of London and the apparent decline of the out-ports in these years did not necessarily ruin those ports, though they did force them to find other ways of earning their living. The urban sector as a whole could not have been as seriously affected as some have suggested, since the damage done in the provinces must to some extent have been balanced by the resultant growth of London.

26

Beyond this point, the theme of urban decay in the period needs to be examined by reference to individual towns. York [29; 72; 99; 100] had the greatest population of any provincial town in 1377; it peaked in about the 1420s and entered a prolonged period of decline between about 1450 and 1530, with a population in the early fifteenth century of around 13,000 dropping to 7000 or so by 1500. The city's governors were prolific in their submission of complaints of poverty to the central government, stating in 1487, for instance, that York then had only half the number of 'good men' it had enjoyed in the past. The decline of York is documented as fully as we could reasonably expect. Analysis of the rolls of newly admitted freemen shows that these self-employed tradesmen dropped in numbers: from about 81 annually in the 1470s to only 52 in the 1520s, the apparent nadir of the decline, before recovering somewhat. The trades followed by these men reveal a reduction in the numbers of merchants and cloth processors over the same period. Studies of urban estates show that rent levels dwindled markedly over this century.

The reasons for this long economic contraction seem to lie in York's problems with its textile industry and its foreign trade. The boom which ended in about 1450 was based on finishing and marketing cloth woven both in the city and in its countryside. This industry was lost to the growing market towns and countryside of the West Riding where, as the mayor explained in 1561, the poor clothworkers could graze their cows and find their fuel more cheaply. Cheap cloth demanded minimal overheads. The loss of most of the cloth tradesmen need not have damaged the export trade in cloth, but competition from Londoners was hard to beat [61], and York lost most of its foreign trade. This was not an inevitable defeat, for Exeter managed to retain the sort of finishing and marketing role that York had once enjoyed. Perhaps the general impoverishment of the north-east coast region, connected with both the stricken wool trade and a general farming recession, lay behind the financial inadequacy of York as the regional capital.

However, York recovered. It was back to third in size among the provincial towns by the 1660s. There are signs of recovery as early as the 1530s and they are clear by 1561 when it became a

27

true provincial capital, with the settlement there of the Council in the North. York recovered in particular by becoming a magnet for the northern gentry who found here a little London of entertainment, shopping, politics, culture and sport. The restructured economy brought new prosperity to many of the late medieval trades which had come through the depression unscathed, for the city's fundamental role as a major regional centre had changed its emphasis but not its essence.

Equally conspicuous in the literature of late medieval decline is the case of Coventry [75; 76]. The third biggest provincial city in 1377, with perhaps 9000 people, and probably more by the early fifteenth century, the brief golden age of the midlands' chief city lasted from possibly 1370 to 1440. By the 1520s subsidy it had fallen to seventh in population, with local surveys showing the city's inhabitants down to about 6000 in 1523; thus its size may have halved between about 1440 and 1550. Unlike York, Coventry staged no immediate recovery. There were indications of difficulties in the city from the middle years of the fifteenth century onwards, but there was something of a recovery in the last two decades of the century before a most serious depression reached its climax. Between October 1520 and June 1523 the number of inhabitants fell by 1500 – a loss of 20 per cent in under three years – while in the latter year a quarter of the houses in the city were standing empty. This situation suggests a crisis of major proportions, associated with epidemics in 1519 and 1525, a slump in the cloth trade, a severe harvest failure with resultant near-famine conditions and unprecedently heavy national tax demands in 1522–5. Here we have well-documented evidence of a grave short-term crisis set in the context of a more obscure long-term decline.

Coventry was in a very odd position, for while it lay in the geographical centre of England, distant from a navigable river and even further from the sea, it functioned to some extent like the other great provincial capitals which were all ports. Coventry used a range of distant harbours to handle the cloth exports and luxury imports which were the basis of its domination of midland trade, but this was a precarious position easily eroded by London. Coventry had become a major cloth producing and processing centre: even in 1523 some 20 per cent of its householders were clothmakers and another 13 per cent were

28

processors, giving a full third of its tradesmen involved in the textile industry.

What seems to have happened is that the production of fine quality broadcloth peaked in the mid-fifteenth century and was excluded from the general upswing in exports in the 1470s. The manufactures of blue thread and of caps were developed to compensate for the failing cloth industry, and Coventry achieved a national reputation for these two quality commodities, but neither provided sufficient employment to absorb all the redundant clothworkers. Meanwhile the city's role as the centre for the wholesale trade of the midlands was slipping. None of these problems was likely to lead to a sudden collapse, and the crisis of the 1520s was probably the result of a malign set of coincidences involving disasters which were mostly natural in origin, for both clothmaking and capping survived. It seems likely that the rapid population loss of 1520–3, followed by some recovery, might have occurred in other towns too, although without leaving any record, but the accidental survival of documented local censuses has made Coventry's long economic contraction look more like a collapse than it really was. It should probably not be taken as 'typical', since so many idiosyncratic circumstances were involved.

Shrewsbury's population did not fall very much between 1377 and 1525 but there was a pronounced reduction by the 1540s [93]. Wealth seems to have dropped more than population, and although the depression lasted longer in Shrewsbury than in some similar towns, its recovery after the 1560s was very striking, with numbers and trade buoyant. Shrewsbury relied on its position on the Welsh border for much of its wealth, for it finished and marketed flannel from Wales, and traded in many commodities flowing between the pastoral west and the arable east. Before the 1460s the town prospered. Wales and the borders had been disturbed by rebellion and lawlessness, so that Shrewsbury was the nearest secure marketplace and source of foodstuffs which were too great a risk to plant at home.

From the 1460s onwards Shrewsbury's markets and shops were increasingly deserted by those who lived further west as they again grew their own cereals and took their business and cloth to market towns nearer home – such as Oswestry and Welshpool – to the detriment of Shrewsbury. This pattern seems to have been reproduced all down the border. Chester complained in 1484 that the Welsh no longer bought their bread and beer there, and Hereford had similar problems in the south. The smaller border market towns to the west of the old commercial centres benefited from the changes, and their growth should be set beside the losses of big towns such as Shrewsbury. Here we have a good example of the restructuring of a regional economy which involved alterations in farming and marketing strategies. This led to a transfer of weight within the urban system rather than to simple urban decline. The circumstances were unique to this area, and should not be readily lumped together with the manifestations of urban decay in other parts of the country.

Bristol was the second largest provincial city in 1377; in the 1520s it maintained this ranking in wealth, and in size too – despite a reduction of population from about 12,000 to 7000 or 8000. This population loss was one of the largest suffered by any city, so Bristol's problems were more serious than at first appears. Through much of the fifteenth century Bristol prospered, with a healthy and growing cloth export trade based on the city's own textile weaving and finishing trades and the output of the flourishing rural industry in its neighbourhood; it had a less significant import trade in wine and other products. The city was hit by the disruption of trade with France and the steady contraction of its cloth industry. By 1486 it was complaining to the crown of decay, referring to unemployment caused by the cloth industry's problems. Even so, clothmaking and especially finishing remained important long after this date, for as late as the 1530s, 18 per cent of the city's new apprentices were employed in the textile crafts; this was no cloth flight on the scale of that at York. More serious was a sudden collapse in cloth exports in the 1490s, as described above. This was chiefly due to competition from London, though Exeter challenged from the south-west too. By 1518 Bristol's government claimed 800 houses abandoned, indicating perhaps a population loss of 3000 to 4000 which the 1520s subsidy figures quoted above would support. Bristol slowly restructured its overseas trade, industries and regional role during the remainder of the sixteenth century, but did not expand rapidly until after 1600, though its status as the capital of its region, and as one of the half-dozen leading English cities was never in doubt.

30

The fate of other major towns with problems conformed to this pattern of a mixture of general similarity and local particularity. Gloucester [72] was an important early medieval town still flourishing early in the 1400s. A river port with some international trade and a cloth industry, Gloucester was also a general regional market centre, specialising in trade across the Welsh border, like Shrewsbury. We first hear pleas of poverty in 1447 and by the 1480s, 300 houses were said to be in decay. Its population slipped from 4250 to 3000 between 1377 and 1524, although ranking in wealth did not decline, suggesting a loss of employment rather than capital. Gloucester is interesting in recovering very rapidly in the first half of the sixteenth century, with a large-scale capping trade developing to provide the mass employment which brought population back up to the 1377 level by 1550. Gloucester ran against the trend again by remaining static in size and wealth during the Elizabethan period. The origins of the city's problems in the second half of the fifteenth century seem unclear, but may be connected with a loss of control over the trade along the Severn to other ports and perhaps some of Shrewsbury's loss of the trans-border commerce. Whatever was wrong, capping soon rescued it.

In the case of Colchester we are fortunate to have a detailed recent study of just this period [74]. The town was quite obscure in 1334 but grew very rapidly after 1350 as a cloth manufacturing town exporting to north-east Europe and Gascony. By 1377 it was the eighth largest town, a status maintained in 1524–5 despite a population decline from about 5600 to 4500. At its peak in around 1410 it was the most important East Anglian cloth centre with up to 8000 people. After this date it lost population, but despite some difficulties its cloth industry appears to have coped well until 1450 at least. Its prosperity was tied to foreign markets rather than its own hinterland, whose agrarian depression may have been a positive help. The town's fortunes after 1450 are poorly documented but do not appear to have involved competition from rurally produced cloth, and although Colchester was shrinking this may have been due to plague and shortage of migrants rather than poverty, for the town cannot be labelled as depressed in the first half of the sixteenth century. As its population fell it may have enjoyed a stabilised or even growing per capita wealth. Thus although by population Colchester can be

31

counted with the declining cloth towns, its wealth may have been more stable, and even its lost population did not reduce its ranking, as other towns at this level shrank more.

Oxford [72] is a relatively straightforward example of undisputed urban decline. Up to the fourteenth century the town had been a major regional centre with important industries and a role in distributing imported luxuries such as wine. During the 1300s the cloth industry died, merchants disappeared, and road and river routes declined. The rural hinterland, once rich due to wool and other agricultural commodities, declined strikingly in the tax lists. This sorry tale was reflected in a reduced tax quota granted in 1442, and in a decline in taxable value from sixth to twenty-sixth in the rankings between 1334 and 1524. By the 1520s the occupations of the townsmen show that it was little more than a large market town with an inflated shopkeeping and service sector catering for the university personnel. As the university expanded later in the sixteenth century Oxford was bound to revive, but for the century 1450–1550 it is a good example of substantiated loss of economic function.

The last of these examples is Southampton [94; 95]. This port went through a series of violent oscillations between boom and slump. It was prosperous in the early 1300s, but the French war and raids ruined it, although it recovered late in the fourteenth century and in the fifteenth it appears, despite some upsets, to have seen a lively commerce. But most of its trade was controlled by Italians (using it as the terminus of their trade with London) and Londoners, both avoiding by this means the dangerous narrow seas around Kent. Southampton's own merchants were few and operated on a small scale, so that the employment and wealth which accrued to the port was slight. During the early years of the sixteenth century Southampton flourished through being, next to London, the chief cloth-shipping port. From the 1530s onwards came collapse as the Italians moved to London and then the Londoners stopped using the port. In 1538/9 only 3 per cent of English cloth exports was shipped from Southampton. By the 1550s the town was extremely depressed and it staged no substantial recovery until after 1600. Here we have a town whose importance rested completely on sea-borne trade, leaving it subject to the instability inherent in such activity; it prospered when many towns were in trouble and conversely declined at the point when many others recovered.

32

This varied catalogue of problem towns will have revealed some factors which several had in common – such as changing foreign trading routes and the vicissitudes of the cloth industry – and a number of factors unique to one region or individual town. Even the chronology of crisis varied, though one can discern a general pattern of prosperity from about 1380 to 1420 or later, with a common trough in the middle of the fifteenth century. Against these examples we must set the towns, often less well documented, which prospered in this period. Some of those towns we have noted as manifesting symptoms of decay during this century also displayed periods of prosperity, and therefore could be partially claimed for the optimist camp – Gloucester and Southampton in the early sixteenth century for instance.

The big towns which on the whole seemed prosperous in this period are a minority. The most important of them was London, although we simply do not know enough about its history at this time to be sure that it grew as consistently as was once assumed. But we do know that its foreign trade grew strongly in this period – at the expense of the provincial ports – and we must assume that at least some of the wealth and population lost by the casualties accrued to the victor. The trend of the time throughout Europe was for capital cities to grow with the strengthening of bureaucratic centralised states, and London was the undisputed centre of government of the most effectively centralised state in Europe. To this vital source of strength it could add its natural economic pre-eminence as the country's greatest port, industrial and aristocratic social and shopping centre, as well as being the capital of the wealthiest province, the south-east. This seems confirmed by the statistical evidence, for London's population grew from perhaps 40,000 in 1377 to maybe 70,000 in 1500 and a firmer figure of well over 100,000 in 1550. This in itself is a much more impressive record than that of any major provincial town, reflected in the fact that the capital's size was only three or four times as big as its nearest rival in 1377 but maybe seven or eight times its rather smaller runner-up in the 1520s. The disparity in wealth was probably even greater. Although we cannot claim that London's progress was unblemished [84; 85; 88] it is hard to see it as an example of anything but general success. Since in the 1520s it was as big as the next fifteen provincial towns put together, it is a very heavy weight to place in the scales. London is so dominant and so obvious that it is

33

easy to take its triumph for granted and overlook its contribution as we sum up the fate of the urban sector as a whole.

If we look at the top of the urban hierarchy, including most of the major regional centres, few were clearly prospering. General success seems confined to the leading provincial city, Norwich, and Exeter, with the possible addition of Canterbury. Norwich's prosperity is borne out by its building boom in the period roughly 1475–1525 and it seems to have derived its eminence from the combination of a successful cloth industry and a role as the capital of a generally prospering region [89]. The city suffered a temporary industrial recession from about 1540 onwards, but its underlying strength as the unchallenged centre of its region seems to have seen it through until its industry revived.

Exeter [78; 79] also flourished from cloth, as a finishing and marketing centre for the Devonshire region. It too was the capital of a prospering region, but it was also a port with the benefit of international commerce. Exeter's rise was sudden, from twenty-second rank in 1377 to third in the 1520s. Its peak came between 1480 and 1510 and it then felt the competition of London and the limitations of its reliance on trade with France. Among the rest of this group, prosperity has been claimed for both Salisbury [28] and Bury St Edmunds [73], in both cases related to the textile industry, while we know insufficient about Newcastle and Canterbury to make a firm judgment. Among the rest of the top 50 towns, we can distinguish some fairly clear groups of rising towns (see Appendices 2–5). Firstly there were the well-known East Anglian clothing towns, such as Hadleigh, Lavenham and Ipswich. Then there were the towns in the rest of southern and south-eastern England, growing either because of cloth (Newbury, Reading) or because they lay in prospering farming and trading regions, with a possible London or clothing connection – Maidstone and Rochester, for instance. Then there were the expanding textile towns of the newly prosperous south-west, Taunton, Tiverton or Barnstaple. Few others can be neatly labelled. Worcester [97], with a self-contained and flourishing broadcloth industry, can be easily explained, but for Chichester, Huntingdon, Lichfield, Barking, Hereford, Northampton and Wisbech we have insufficient local studies to do more than guess. Many of these towns were rather small, but that is what might be expected of up-and-coming towns at any time, and especially

34

when economic change is rapid. The regional factor is certainly conspicuous here, with nearly all the successful towns situated in the south.

This is perhaps the point at which to consider the thesis of a general urban crisis in the middle years of the sixteenth century, from perhaps 1520 to 1570 [30; 76]. This concept fits in well with the idea of a national mid-sixteenth century crisis, characterised by political instability, religious indecision, social stress (the peasant risings of 1547–9) and economic troubles – currency manipulation, acute price inflation and bad harvests. It would be difficult for all this to fail to have an urban impact. Apart from the example of specific towns, such as our old friends Coventry, York, Lincoln or Winchester, two classes of evidence are brought forward to support the thesis of general urban decay. The first is the comparison of population totals between the subsidy of 1524/5 and the survey of household numbers of 1563. Unfortunately the problem of inflating the numbers of taxpayers of the 1520s into a population estimate is unsettled and the meaning of the 1563 survey is even more uncertain. So there are little generally accepted statistical data reflecting urban conditions during the middle years of the century.

The second class of evidence is contained in Acts of Parliament and polemical literature. Amongst a certain group of contemporary intellectuals, including what used to be called the Commonwealth Men, it was taken for granted that towns were in difficulties, short of people, and falling down. Starkey's *Dialogue between Pole and Lupsett* [71] of the early 1530s, talks of towns having been 'much better inhabited and much more replenished with people than they be now', leading to houses which are 'plain ruinate and decayed', and goes on to make similar statements about country villages as well [71, 49]. It is hard to assess whether these commentators were able to form a sufficiently wide and objective view. John Hales, one of the leading propagandists for this school, was very closely associated with Coventry and may well be excessively influenced by his experience of one of the greatest urban casualties. Their thinking is probably reflected in the statutes of the period [53], at its most typical in the measures attempting to discourage rural competition, such as the Act of 1534 which confined clothmaking to the towns of Worcestershire and the statute of 1555 which claimed that the towns would 'come very shortly to utter destruction, ruin and decay' if village shopkeepers were not suppressed. What these Acts undoubtedly reveal is the presence of a pressure group in parliament trying to strengthen the powers and wealth of towns. Whether its claims were based on substantial truth or not is less certain, but parliament was undeniably prone to the assertion of urban self-interest because an expanding majority of its members was elected by boroughs.

It is difficult to assess the idea of a crisis at this time. How do we disentangle the symptoms of general crisis from those of specifically urban problems? Lack of reliable statistical data makes assessment of the literary evidence particularly difficult. It is also hard to comprehend why this period should see the lowest point in the fortunes of towns when one would expect it to come rather earlier – in the mid-fifteenth century when we know that population, prices and exports were at a low ebb. By the 1530s, and probably earlier, population was swinging upwards, as were agricultural prices, while the cloth export boom was in full swing and still had twenty years to run.

5 The Problems of Evidence

Most of the major classes of evidence which underpin discussion of the crucial phase of the alleged urban decline, that is the period roughly 1420 to 1560, have in recent years been subjected to re-examination. The result has often been to undermine those earlier conclusions which were based on a too-straightforward reading of the documents. Nothing is quite what it seems; ambiguity is everywhere.

A prime example of this truth is presented by the evidence of taxation. Here it seemed we might find some hard facts. W. G. Hoskins first produced lists of the leading provincial towns at various dates, ranked in descending order of either size or wealth. For our period he hit on the three great taxes of 1334, 1377 and 1524–5, showing which towns had gained or lost wealth or population between these dates [24, *174–8*]. Modified versions of these rankings appear in Appendices 1–4 of this pamphlet. However, this evidence, though it showed that some notable changes were apparently taking place in the relative positions of individual towns, did not indicate whether towns as a class could be said to be suffering impoverishment.

In 1962 A. R. Bridbury analysed the data of 1334 and 1524–5 to support his controversial thesis of urban vigour in the later middle ages [28]. His figures apparently showed that most towns were paying far more in taxation in 1524 than they had done in 1334, and that their share of the national tax yield had more than doubled, from about 6.5 per cent of the total assessed value of a group of 28 counties to about 15 per cent of the total paid in 1524. Although Bridbury apparently does not believe that this necessarily proves that the towns grew in wealth between these two dates, his figures for individual towns arrange them in a hierarchy which fits well with what we know from other sources. This represents one of the chief problems for the advocates of the thesis of urban decline: how can such apparent general buoyancy be squared with their belief in widespread decay?

Further work and discussion of the tax date have continued, with S. Rigby and J. Hadwin the most prominent participants in a debate which has now reached a stalemate [44–48]. It has been suggested by those arguing for decline that Bridbury's statistics can be explained away if we assume that both country and town may have declined in wealth, with the countryside losing more, thus making the towns appear richer. More promisingly, Hadwin argues that the towns were seriously under-assessed in 1334, so that when their true riches were revealed in 1524, their tax yield seems to increase. However, even the most indulgent assumption of urban under-assessment in 1334 can only bring country and town back to rough parity, and no one has yet contorted the figures to support a thesis of declining urban wealth *vis-à-vis* the rural areas. Even if we cannot now use the subsidies to make a clear case for urban growth, they certainly remain a major obstacle for the pessimist school.

The basic problem in coping with the tax data is that we are dealing with two assessments separated by 190 years during which the population of the country as a whole fell by a half, with consequent radical structural changes. To add to this, we do not know what relationship the sums noted down by the tax collectors bore to the real wealth of the communities concerned at either date. The tax of 1334 was entirely, and that of 1524–5 very largely, assessed on the value of movable goods, but it seems that in 1334 the objects needed for a farmer to support himself – a cart or plough for instance – were exempt from taxation; did similar conventions operate in the 1520s? At both dates most of the tax was paid by a small minority of the population, and changes in the way their assets were assessed may have been very considerable. Comparisons rest on the assumption that about the same proportion of wealth was skimmed off on each occasion, but one suspects that the 1520s subsidy dug uniquely deep into the pockets of Englishmen; no attempt to make the tax record tell us whether towns were growing wealthier or poorer can succeed until this point is cleared up.

A comparison which has not hitherto been explored very thoroughly is that between the population levels indicated by

38

taxation documents. For this purpose we have the poll tax of 1377 and the 1524–5 subsidy (see Appendix 5). Both records must be processed before we can use them for demographic purposes. The poll tax data must be inflated to allow for children, evasion and poverty, and a multiplier of about 1.9 is generally accepted as providing an approximation to the total population [15, 14, 68]. Unfortunately the taxes of 1524–5 are more difficult to handle, but a multiplier in the area of 6.5 seems not unreasonable, at least as a basis for argument [93; 76, 12; 74, 201; 98, 368; 88, 176]. It would indicate a total English population of about 2.6 million for the 1520s, about 10 per cent below that of 1377, which fits well with recent estimates.

Appendix 5 shows the results of this exercise, covering the leading 50 towns at both dates. This provides us with a list of 57 towns with reasonable data, and another five without adequate records for the 1520s. The main group of 57 may be divided into three sub-sections: one set of 24 shrinks in size without much doubt; the second group conversely expands, and contains almost the same number of towns, while the third set of 11 could move in either direction within reasonable margins of error. This gives us a full list in which the shrinking towns are roughly balanced in number by those which are expanding – there is no clear support for either side in the controversy.

If, however, we total the populations concerned we find that in the base list of 57, total population falls from 191,000 to 168,000 between 1377 and the 1520s, the result of a loss of 45,000 in the declining towns being only partially compensated by a rise of 22,000 in the rest. This amounts to a loss of about 12 per cent of the total population of these towns, though if the 1520s multiplier were to be increased quite modestly to 7.4, the loss would disappear.

However, a general loss of about 10 per cent is revealed if we apply the same multipliers of 1.9 and 6.5 to the total populations of all the counties with reasonable data, so that all that has happened is that the towns have drifted downwards to about the same extent as the countryside, and therefore no de-urbanisation has taken place. Furthermore we have only counted the larger provincial towns. Above them lies London, which may well have grown, and below them spreads a prospect of hundreds of market towns which are often thought to have been holding their own in this period. That this may be true is indicated by a comparison of the urban structure in the two years concerned. In the 1520s the smallest towns in our sample, ranked at about 50, were about 20 per cent bigger than their 1377 equivalents; this might suggest that some of the population loss in the big towns was being mopped up by the small ones.

If we look at individual towns in these tables, the notorious decliners, York, Lincoln, Coventry and the rest, and the familiar success stories such as Norwich, Exeter and Reading, all appear where we should expect them to be. A particular feature which emerges here is that the loss of urban population is concentrated in relatively few places. York, Lynn, Bristol and Coventry between them account for nearly 22,000 of the losses, and with the addition of Beverley, Boston and Lincoln these seven towns are the only ones which appear to have lost more than 1600 people apiece. This would suggest that towns which appear repeatedly in the literature are conspicuous not because they are the tip of an iceberg but rather because they amount to the full list of major casualties and reappear because there are few others to exemplify their class. On the other hand it must be conceded that the most important towns of 1377 were hit very hard, for 9 of the top 10 and 16 of the top 20 end up with smaller populations in 1524. Population loss spread so widely amongst this group of dominant provincial centres must be regarded as a significant feature in its own right, even though other towns may have been growing to compensate for much of this loss.

A comparison of tax returns from the fourteenth and sixteenth centuries may also provide us with a regional perspective of changes in wealth and population. Comparisons on a county basis of wealth in 1334 and 1524–5 (Map 1) show changes rather more dramatic than the urban figures suggest. Three broad areas may be identified here. The first lies in the south-east, with its rising wealth centred on London, and presumably connected with the access of these counties to the London food market and the growth of the cloth industry. The second can be found in the strikingly expanding south-west, with Cornwall, Devon and Somerset, Dorset and Wiltshire all amongst the fastest growers. Thirdly there is a zone of contraction, in some cases precipitous, affecting some of the wealthiest areas of fourteenth century England – Oxfordshire, Norfolk, Bedfordshire, Cambridgeshire

40

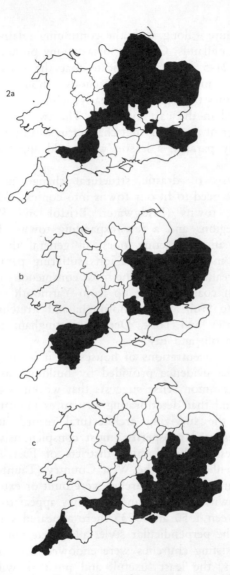

Map 2 *Changes in distribution of taxpaying population
1377–1524/5 in 32 English counties.*
■ *= Upper half; a = 1377; b = 1524/5; c = growth
rate 1377–1524/5.*
*Major towns excluded. Calculated as taxpayers per sq.
mile.*

and Lincolnshire – along with the continuing relative poverty of much of the midlands. Changes in taxpaying population between 1377 and 1524–5 (Map 2) indicate that the expansion of the south-west is much less conspicuous, though that of the south-east comes through more clearly, while the area of greatest loss is centred in the east midlands. The two approaches bring out the danger of assuming that changes in wealth and population are necessarily parallel, a lesson we should apply to the towns too.

This analysis of drastic structural change in the regions underlines the need to fit our towns into context. Although there are declining towns (Bridgwater, Bristol and Plymouth) in prospering regions and a few expanding towns (Lichfield and Huntingdon) in contracting ones, in general the towns with problems lie in agricultural regions suffering parallel losses of people and wealth, of which the most conspicuous is the tract of the north-east coast running up from Yarmouth through Lynn and Boston to Hull and Scarborough, and stretching inland to include Beverley and York, Derby, Nottingham and Leicester, Stamford, Lincoln and Ely.

Towns are concentrations of houses, so it is not unreasonable to turn to the evidence provided by buildings as evidence of prosperity. Common sense suggests that wealth is a prerequisite of building and that deteriorating structures indicate poverty. If we turn to the surviving architectural record, it appears to indicate widespread prosperity, most conspicuously in the glorious churches of the clothing districts of East Anglia (Long Melford, Lavenham) and the West Country (Taunton, Chipping Camden). Many of these churches were built or extended around 1500 when towns like York and Coventry appear to have been in trouble. Between 1350 and 1535 there appeared some 1100 new churches in the perpendicular style, all replete with towers, and some 2300 existing churches were endowed with heightened or rebuilt towers, the least 'useful' and most showily decorative element in church building. Surely all this activity must point to prosperity?

In many cases it does, but because there are so many examples of building in towns that we know were in difficulties, we cannot take this activity at its face value. In Exeter the headquarters of its government, the Guildhall, was rebuilt in 1468, confirming

42

what we know of the city's prosperity. Yet York did the same in the late 1450s when it was entering its decline (though could the city fathers have known?). Many towns allowed their walls and gates to deteriorate, but was this because they now felt more secure? Much showy building owes its origin to small groups of rich individuals, or even to just one person. The churches of Tiverton and Cullompton were endowed with splendid new aisles each provided by the wealthiest clothier in the place, and this coincides with genuine prosperity. But such enormously wealthy individuals could be found in decayed communities. Troubled Coventry, for example, was the home of Richard Marler, grocer, one of the four richest men in the whole of the 1524–5 tax lists.

In many towns, both declining and otherwise, the surviving domestic buildings speak of rising standards of living with wealth devoted to display and enhanced creature comforts such as glass windows and tiled roofs. One recent writer has concluded that if we relied solely on the evidence of standing buildings we should assume that the age was 'a period of unparalleled prosperity' [6, 204]; yet these buildings survive only because no one replaced them in later centuries, so that the distribution of this evidence reflects the prosperity or poverty of these towns in the modern as well as the late medieval period.

Classic evidence of urban decay was until recently accepted in the so-called Rebuilding Acts passed by parliament between 1536 and 1544 [31, 62–3]. These acts seem to be based on a statute of 1534 which allowed Norwich, which had suffered a serious fire in 1507, to deal with the 'many' vacant sites by ordering the owners to wall or rebuild their properties within a set period; if they refused the city could confiscate them and rebuild. The series of Rebuilding Acts list some 80 towns in measures which follow a standard form, referring to the offence and danger presented by many dilapidated buildings and vacant plots near main streets. If owners failed to repair or rebuild, town governments could confiscate the site and themselves rebuild. Here it seems we have hard evidence of extensive physical decay widespread throughout the country, and inclusion in one of the acts has been considered sufficient to brand a particular town as suffering from the prevailing economic malaise.

Yet when the population of most towns fell substantially with the impact of plague after 1349, there must have been a very

43

extensive contraction in their built-up area and housing stock, leaving patches of dereliction and many vacant plots. The acts list towns which we know to have been prosperous at the time – like Worcester, Exeter, Ipswich and Taunton – as well as most of the notorious seats of decay. It appears that town authorities saw that these measures provided them with handy powers, whether their predicament was serious or not, and that the draft acts were made available to any town with members of parliament willing to include its name [53]. Of the 50 largest towns in the 1520s, 20 do not appear in the Acts, and these omissions must be explained by the fact that nearly all of them had no parliamentary representation at the time. Thus the lists of towns in the acts reflect constitutional as much as physical conditions. The texts of the acts refer to the 'many *beautiful* houses' which had disappeared, and their proximity to the main streets, as well as the danger to passers-by as if it were the conspicuous nature of these eyesores and the danger they presented which was the real point at issue rather than any sense of whole tracts of towns falling into ruin.

The acts also specify that notice of impending confiscation must be served on plots by an on-site proclamation, ignoring the use of the courts, which suggests that a frequent problem was the absence of any known owner on whom a writ could be served. During the long period of physical contraction after the first plague attack, the identity of owners must sometimes have been lost, so here was a useful way of re-establishing ownership as a necessary prelude to any kind of action. Where we can trace in the town records what measures were actually taken as a result of these new powers, the number of properties concerned is very small, usually a handful and at the most less than twenty, as in Coventry in 1541. The 1534 Act for Norwich seems to have been aimed at no more than a couple of dozen plots not rebuilt after the 700 houses burnt in 1507 [89, 23]. If town centres were really so full of these sites there ought to be more evidence of action. If town governments were to rebuild (for they forfeited the confiscated sites themselves if they failed to do so) this presupposes a healthy demand for housing. So the acts reflect the attractions for town governments of inexpensive means of adding to their estates while tidying up prominent street frontages and gaining some of the powers previously granted by expensive private acts for street improvement. If they tell us much about

44

the general state of buildings, it is that by their date, dereliction had become a problem susceptible to treatment.

If these documents give no clear indication of the state of urban housing, perhaps archaeology could give an unbiased view. And it does, up to a point, in confirming the reliability of what we think we already know. Excavations in Winchester [98] have confirmed the general pattern of poverty and contraction indicated by the documents, while archaeological work in Norwich shows a building boom between about 1470 and 1530 in which the housing stock was modernised; but then we already knew that Norwich was relatively prosperous. The problem with archaeological evidence is that it comes from a restricted range of places, cannot often date structures sufficiently closely to add to the historical record, and has been destroyed on many main street frontages of major provincial towns by the rebuilding consequent upon continued or revived prosperity.

Rather more helpful has been the intensive study of documentary sources in particular towns, especially deeds and rentals, sometimes combined with surveys of surviving structures and excavation. Town rentals in Bury St Edmunds [73] reveal that some central areas of the town were being abandoned, while others in the suburbs were growing. When the Abbey was dissolved the central housing property which it owned was very dilapidated, yet Bury's cloth industry had prospered in the fifteenth century. It appears that activity was shifting from one locality within the town to another and the monks were neglecting their estates towards the end of their existence.

The intensive study of property records of all kinds in a small area of Cheapside [84; 85] in London provides evidence which is equally difficult to interpret. Here land values and the intensity of occupation reached a peak in about 1300 and then declined consistently until the 1550s. Some sites were left vacant and on others a single building replaced several. Conventional opinion has assumed that London always prospered, so the apparent slackness in demand for housing in the early sixteenth century, when its cloth exports were shooting ahead, is especially baffling. But some districts in suburban London do indicate growth by the later 1400s [88], suggesting that expansion may have begun at the periphery before it spread to the centre. Behind the Cheapside housing data lie indications of basic changes in the trades pursued

45

in Cheapside, but also in the nature of businesses, for the amazingly small-scale activity in 1300, with thousands of traders operating from chests or standing room in buildings like bazaars, was replaced by 1500 by a much smaller number of considerably more substantial businesses.

The ambiguity of so much of our evidence is well illustrated from Gloucester [55; 72; 80], where difficulties were making themselves felt by 1447 when the city petitioned the crown for a reduction in its dues because recent epidemics had caused the abandonment of many houses in the town. This would seem to be fair evidence of urban decline, except for the survival of a local survey of 1455 – only eight years later – which lists all the properties in the town. It reveals that of the 700 holdings listed, a mere 6 were described as 'ruined' or 'decayed'; on the other hand 48 were termed 'new', though this term could be applied to buildings erected up to a dozen or so years earlier. There is evidence both of overcrowding and of considerable investment by landlords in house building and renewal. Gloucester stands revealed as making very suspect claims to the crown, yet the survey does reveal aspects consistent with a measure of decay as well as prosperity.

Although such surveys are very rare, we do have quite extensive records left by urban landlords. These rentals and accounts have revealed a rather dismal picture. In York [29; 72; 99; 100] several estates reveal house rents sliding downward during the course of the fifteenth century by about a half, though in at least one case they were increasing again by the 1540s. Confirmatory data come from Cheapside in London [84], where a weak upturn did not appear until 1500–10, Westminster [88] (slipping from 1410–20 onwards but recovering, like other London suburban areas before 1500), Hull [54], where rents fell from about 1450 until they were about halved by 1530, Oxford and Canterbury [51]. Physical decay, that is the actual dereliction of buildings, was uncommon; much money was spent on repairs (suggesting an underlying optimism). The principal problem lay with weakness of demand from would-be tenants, who were able to bargain their rents downward, rather than the deterioration of house fabric. We cannot explain away this dismal impression by suggesting that the records of private owner-occupiers would reveal a different story because most townsmen leased their homes, usually from large institutional landowners. However,

46

part of the fall of rental income may come from the rent reductions agreed when the obligation to repair houses was passed from landlord to tenant, thus distorting the apparent significance of the accounts. And it is worth considering that while falling rents were bad news for landlords, they suited tenants very well, and represented a potential improvement in their living standards. Much of this evidence comes from towns which we already know were in trouble, not from the many towns shown by the 1520s subsidy to be growing or holding their own.

It would then appear that in many towns demand for housing was slack, though the reasons for this have yet to be proved. However, the rental evidence fails to substantiate some of the allegations of physical deterioration which were made at the time. The bishop of Lincoln in 1483 blamed the 'sloth and negligence' of landlords for the trend to 'extreme decay and ruin' evident in towns; perhaps such observers exaggerated, or took the experience of the few places they knew well to be a universal one. Certainly John Leland, one of the few writers we do know to be capable of taking a general view, who has left us his accounts of very extensive travels through every region, referred to physical decay remarkably rarely, despite the strange and often-repeated assertion that he noticed widespread ruin.

A large class of evidence is supplied by petitions and complaints alleging distress submitted by towns to either the crown or parliament. Often these centred on pleas for the reduction of the fee farm, which was the sum of money which the crown assigned to be paid to it by a town when it received a charter granting a measure of self-government. Towns in trouble petitioned the crown for reductions in this sum when they considered themselves impoverished, and most of these pleas, with the supporting arguments, have been preserved. It is impossible to deny that some of these wails were justified. In Shrewsbury, for instance, a fee farm of £30 was reduced by both Richard III and Henry VII on the basis of a decline in the town government's income; our knowledge of the town accounts shows that this was true, as tolls on trade had fallen, although the municipality was still able to balance its books.

In other cases the resources which were earmarked for paying the fee farm were undoubtedly reduced. Gloucester's bailiffs petitioned in 1447 that they had to pay £20 of the £65 due to the

47

crown from their own pockets because the income they received was inadequate. This may well have been the case, but the bailiffs' sole financial function was to collect certain monies and use them to pay the farm, while the remainder of the municipal income and expenditure was managed by other officials who might have been under less pressure. This was characteristic of their less than frank approaches to the crown, for in 1505 they were claiming that their 'certain' income was only £9. This was technically correct since this was the only fixed sum, but there were other substantial revenues available which happened to vary annually. These selective, and in many cases deliberately misleading, petitions were common. Winchester claimed in 1440 and repeated on more than one later occasion that it had lost 17 parish churches, 11 streets and 987 houses over the previous fifty or more years [98]. The church total is about right, but the total of houses is impossibly high when we check it against a local survey of 1417. Another misleading feature of these petitions is their grossly overwrought language. Every modest change is 'like to come very shortly to utter destruction, ruin and decay'. Such was the standard phraseology of any partisan argument of the age and we should never take it as a literal truth. Yet, when we have discounted all this distortion, it appears very likely that there was some sort of a case behind many of these pleas.

However, an inability to pay dues by particular officials may not reveal a poor town government, since the municipality might, for instance, have moved money out of accounts which could be tapped by the crown. And a poor town government does not presuppose an impoverished town, for taxpayers were adept at keeping their governments as poor as possible. Certainly the crown instituted local enquiries to check on these protestations, but we cannot be sure that central government was genuinely interested in real facts, for successive royal governments in the fifteenth century were desperate to buy political support from the towns by playing up to the charade put up by the municipalities [70]. Richard III was especially prone to these manoeuvres, making personal visits both to Gloucester and York at which he ostentatiously granted remission of their dues. That politics lay behind some of these grants is clear from the case of Leicester, which for technical reasons paid no fee farm to the crown which could be reduced to win the town's support; instead it had to be

48

given an annuity by both Edward IV and Henry VII in gratitude for imaginary services rendered. These awards cost the crown relatively little, especially as some of the sums had already been granted to courtiers and officials so that their cancellation affected only these persons.

Thus evidence which at first sight seems to be detailed and sound, pointing to extensive decline, can be shown on closer examination to be much less convincing. Undoubtedly behind the smokescreen there were towns with genuine difficulties, but many of them turn out to be the same familiar list of frequently repeated names which already appear among the documented cases of decay shown up by taxation and other evidence. No one has listed the towns which do not complain, but we ought mentally to set this negative evidence against the oft-repeated hyperbole.

Closely linked with this claimed inability to pay taxes is the theme of the alleged refusal of leading townsmen to take municipal office. Virtually all towns were governed by small groups of wealthy citizens, co-opting new officials from the richer townsmen not already holding office. It has been claimed that a symptom of urban decline was an increasing reluctance of these leading citizens to take office, principally because they feared the expense of paying from their own pockets when official revenues fell short [29; 30]. This is often suggested by towns when applying for reductions in crown dues. The issue was first raised in the case of York, but there closer examination [38] has revealed that the number of cases is not great and that usually the council nominated men it knew to be ineligible in order to raise money from fining their predictable refusal. Those genuinely qualified to serve were on the whole willing to do so. This phenomenon was not all confined to towns in trouble, for the governors of London regularly nominated men who were not potential candidates as a disguised tax, fining 13 men in succession in 1591; at that time and place, decline was out of the question.

Connected with this theme is the allegation that town governments indulged in conspicuous display and wasteful expense which increased the burdens on weakened economies. Certainly late medieval towns enjoyed an annual round of public ceremonial which must have been expensive, though rather more of time than of money. Perhaps they knew their own business best, and if they behaved like this they were well aware of the underlying wealth in their communities. Pomp and display were essential to bolster authority at all levels, from the monarchy downwards, and doubly so for the rulers of urban communities without armed force to support them in a violent and stressful period. Ceremony strengthened power and, within reason, was the last subject for penny-pinching economies.

6 Expansion and Decline 1540–1640

The problems of fifteenth century towns must be seen against a nationwide background of demographic stagnation and economic uncertainty, but from about 1540 we enter a period characterised by an expanding population and a more clearly successful economy [9; 10]. Population began to grow at some point between 1470 and 1520; by 1640 the national total had roughly doubled, transforming the position of the towns, which were now assured of an abundant source of immigrants from an increasingly overpopulated countryside. With the expanded supply of people, wages fell and labour costs dropped, thus solving one of the most serious of urban economic problems. Twice as many mouths had to be fed, so agricultural prices rose sharply; farming prospered, and so country people could afford more urban goods and services. Equally important was the transformation of the old agrarian economy, local, small-scale and inclined towards mere subsistence, into a new commercialised and market-oriented system, with local specialisation and much inter-regional trade in large-scale surpluses. These developments could only enrich the many towns through which much of this trade in rural commodities was unavoidably funnelled.

Other trends were less conducive to urban growth. The long boom in cloth exports came to an end when the Antwerp market crashed in 1551 and a long struggle to find alternative markets ensued. There was a revival in export markets between about 1610 and 1620, but further difficulties brought on by continental warfare and other problems led to crises in the 1620s and decline in the 1630s. However, by 1640 there were signs that the instability inherent in over-reliance on exporting cloth to the near continent was giving way to a healthier system as colonial trade and new routes to fresh markets were opened up. The excessive domination of foreign trade by London was reduced, and by the early 1600s provincial ports were handling a quarter of total cloth

51

exports. However, cloth production remained depressed for most of the Elizabethan period, though expanding domestic demand may have helped to fill part of the gap for the clothmakers.

Traditional woollen cloths were increasingly difficult to sell as cheaper textiles in lighter weights came into demand. English clothiers eventually responded by producing new types of cloth, typically those termed 'New Draperies', which sold well, but the period of readjustment was a long one and was only just being completed when in the 1620s and 30s continental demand plummeted in war and depression. Those towns which were involved in textiles were nearly all affected by long-term contraction in the later sixteenth century, followed by alternating extremes of boom and slump after 1605. If towns specialising in the traditional product could not adapt, they often declined, like Newbury and Reading [90], though for those which could adjust to the New Draperies – such as Norwich [89] and Colchester in the east and many of the Devonshire towns around Exeter in the west – prosperity was restored.

Apart from the problems of the cloth industry, other factors were more clearly encouraging for the towns [21]. The growth of centralised administration increased the functions of both London and the county capitals. A conspicuous innovation in the activity of the state was much greater investment in the armed forces, especially the navy, so it is not surprising to find that naval bases like Chatham and Portsmouth grew rapidly. The most important social development of the period was the growth in numbers, wealth and power of the gentry. Many towns found a new role as centres for the social, political, shopping and entertainment activities of this group, and their close allies in the professions – doctors, lawyers, teachers – who were natural town residents and were growing in importance in these years.

The most influential analysis of urban fortunes for the period 1540–1640 has been provided by Clark and Slack [19; 20]. Theirs is a pessimistic picture. For them the widespread urban decay of the mid-sixteenth century was followed by a period of unrelenting general difficulty for most of the middling and large towns right up to 1700, at best 'able to earn no more than temporary remission in their general decline' [20, 32]. Their economies were basically unstable, they were damaged by low demand for their goods and services from a population impoverished by low wages

52

and high food prices and above all they were racked by periodic disasters – plague and other epidemics, fire and famine and the destruction and disruption of the Civil War – and the constant debilitating tide of immigrant poor. Only the ordinary run of market towns escaped this litany of mishaps, to enjoy a prosperity which cannot counterbalance the misery of their larger brethren.

However, few specialists writing in the wake of this synthesis have accepted it without qualification, and it is significant that both of the recent general surveys of the economic history of the period [9; 10] have opted for a more cheerful view of the towns after 1570, admitting that there are some depressed areas and serious problems, but preferring a general picture of substantial, if unspectacular progress, and certainly not accepting that the concept of general urban decline has much validity after 1570. Two points seem widely accepted. The first is that the market towns prospered in this century, their golden age. Expanding agricultural production and incomes were serviced by these towns, which consequently grew in size and wealth, though not in numbers until after 1660. The other area of agreement is the phenomenal growth in the size, wealth, importance and influence of London, which is now estimated to have contained over its whole built-up area 120,000 inhabitants in 1550 and 375,000 by 1650 [83]. There is no quarrelling with the undisputed success story of the capital, by 1600 much larger than the aggregate population (at about 130,000) of all the 17 provincial towns with at least 5000 inhabitants.

If we look back at the Clark and Slack thesis, it seems to over-stress the difficulties faced by the larger towns in this period. It suggests that growth was actually harmful, since it is said to lead to mounting problems of all kinds, and especially of poor relief. Yet population size is the only measure of success that we have. Although the problems of poor relief bulk large in town records, the burden does not seem to have been particularly depressing; urban economies paid much less to national taxation than they had done under Henry VIII, and outbreaks of violence were surprisingly infrequent. The poor provided a reservoir of cheap labour which guaranteed relatively low wage costs for urban businesses. A recent survey of the problem of poverty [11] finds the wretchedly poor to have been a smaller proportion of

53

urban society than used to be believed, while the latest study of sixteenth century London [87] considers that its poverty problem was relatively small and easily managed and its society harmonious and either not subject to those acute stresses which Clark and Slack considered so devastating, or able to cope with them without lasting harm. The crises of fire, famine and plague have been seen as very damaging. But fires were not common until after 1640 and were confined to limited areas of the country, while the towns that were affected generally recovered with surprising ease. Famine was receding and was more of a rural problem. As for plague, an admittedly serious threat, it was not as frequent a visitor as formerly and once epidemics had run their course towns revealed a remarkable resilience, especially as it was the superfluous poor who died and could now be easily restocked from the countryside [18].

If we are to generalise about the experience of early modern towns then we must turn to the rankings based on the hearth tax of 1662 (Appendix 3). This reveals a general stability amongst the larger towns: the five leading towns of 1524–5, Bristol, Exeter, Newcastle, Norwich and York are still there, although their relative positions have altered a little. Of the top 36 towns in 1662, all were already represented in the biggest 40 in the 1520s, with the exception of Portsmouth, Leeds and Chatham. Within this overall stability – consistent with the idea that this is a period of readjustment and strengthening of the existing urban systen – it is possible to discern some clear trends.

One was the reassertion of the natural position of a number of regional centres which had lain under a temporary cloud (or were misleadingly assessed) in the 1520s. Great Yarmouth, Shrewsbury, probably Chester, Lynn, Nottingham and Derby all fall into this category. Oxford and Cambridge both recovered from their misfortunes, aided by the revived activity of their universities as both the Reformation and the Renaissance swelled the ranks of their students. Both probably restored their regional commercial role too, connected, as in a number of other cases, with a recovery of some of the old wealth of farming in their localities. A resurgence of northern prosperity was also evident in the recovery of York, Hull and Nottingham to their former importance. Part of this may be an illusion caused by under-assessment in the 1520s which made their late medieval decline

54

seem worse than it actually was, but certainly there had been an evening up of the distribution of the nation's wealth which had been so distorted towards the south in the fifteenth century. The recovery of Hull [72] was especially noteworthy and reflected its role as the shipping point for cloth from the West Riding industry whose growth is marked by the appearance of Leeds in the rankings. The declining towns in the rankings were mostly connected with the troubled cloth industry, especially where the old broadcloth had not been superseded by the newer types. Reading and Newbury were the most prominent here but also St Albans, Bury St Edmunds, Salisbury, Colchester and Taunton, along with a number of smaller places in East Anglia and the West Country had lost wealth or inhabitants.

Population levels are the best absolute measure of change. Between 1525 and 1600 the total population of the leading 17 provincial towns rose from about 85,000 to about 130,000, and perhaps to 160,000 by 1640, since growth seems to have been faster in the seventeenth century. Three of these towns (Canterbury, Colchester and Salisbury) had put on little growth by 1600 but the rest had grown strongly, in particular Newcastle, flourishing as the capital of a growing region and more particularly as the source of London's coal. Plymouth was another flourishing port. The roughly 50–60 per cent growth shown by the whole group was only modestly behind the increase shown by the national population total, and would probably be higher if we had figures for the medium sized and smaller market towns, where growth, outside London, was probably most pronounced.

Some towns were in difficulties; there always would be, especially when there was substantial economic change in progress. Many textile towns experienced depression, though they were capable of recovery. Norwich worsteds were difficult to sell from the 1530s onwards [89] and the survey of the poor of 1570 revealed a worrying level of under-employment. From 1565 onward refugee clothworkers from the Low Countries introduced the New Draperies and Norwich steadily recovered its old prosperity and then flourished, doubling its 1525 population to over 20,000 in 1640, and maintaining its status as the leading provincial city throughout. Gloucester is an example of a middling rank city for which there was no rescue [72]. It grew very little, if at all, over this period, since both its broadcloth and its capping crafts were depressed. It could find no adequate substitute industrial product and failed to develop very substantially as a shopping and social centre for the rural upper classes. But its decline, as with similar towns, was a relative rather than an absolute affair, for Gloucester remained stationary while others advanced. Of the smaller failing towns we have the example of Stafford [96], where the population fell steadily during most of the seventeenth century due to an inability to exploit the potential advantages of a county town and market centre. Plague and harvest failure, as in Gloucester, punctuated the town's history, but their effects should be seen against a background of endemic economic weakness which made these disasters the agent by which population was scaled down to match the contracting economic base. The problem lay in failure to compete with neighbouring towns; the opportunities existed but were taken by others, and in this, apart from the case of some of the declining textile towns, we probably have the principal factor behind the minority of failing towns before 1640.

A loss of industrial function has often been mentioned in connection with urban decline, usually with reference to cloth-making. In part this was because cloth was so prominent as a provider of mass employment and as a source of showy profit in boom times, that other forms of manufacture were overshadowed. Of course some towns continued to profit from cloth after 1550, but reliance on a single industry which was so liable to competition and disruption injected a permanent element of instability into the urban structure. The century after 1550 saw that instability reduced by the development of many alternative sources of employment in urban manufactures, aided by the strength of domestic demand and the supply of cheap labour provided by migrants from the countryside. This healthy process occurred in many country towns of middling size, often involving the development of a specialist product based on locally available raw materials and catering for a relatively distant market. Oxford developed a gloving trade, and Northampton specialised in shoes, both supplying the metropolitan market, while Wigan was a centre for pewter and Walsall for horse harness. As part of this process we might note the development

56

of market towns with prominent industrial specialisms in previously under-urbanised regions, such as Birmingham with its metal goods, Sheffield for edge-tools and Manchester as a centre for Lancashire textiles. These towns were already drawing away from their neighbours by 1640 and we can see here, as elsewhere, the clear roots of the urban growth which was to be such a feature of the period after 1660.

7 Conclusion

In the wider perspective of continental Europe, the current literature on towns in the fifteenth and sixteenth centuries reveals little trace of that conspicuous urban decline which the pessimist school finds in England. One authority considers that the period 1400–1800 was for European towns a time of 'trendless fluctuation' with 'population declines, small increases, and periods of stability, albeit in fluctuating rhythms' [23, 8–9]. De Vries's study of the larger European towns (those with more than 10,000 inhabitants) reveals gentle expansion in the later middle ages [22]. After 1500, urban decline is not a major issue until the Mediterranean cities contract in the seventeenth century. In England De Vries finds a slow but consistent urbanisation from 1500 to 1800. But he is only concerned with the very peak of the English urban hierarchy and on the continent population probably increased much earlier in the fifteenth century than in England, a circumstance which would have encouraged earlier urban growth. However, we must acknowledge that there appears to be no continental parallel for general English urban decline until the seventeenth century. De Vries does provide some support for an element of the English experience by suggesting that instability on the continent seemed to be connected most commonly with loss of industry to the countryside.

The example of eighteenth century Japan provides us with an interesting parallel [22, 245]. There population was static and foreign trade minimal; when economic expansion took place in the agricultural sector, higher incomes led to a demand for goods and services which the towns could not provide because they lacked the labour, since they could not attract sufficient migrants. Instead, manufacturers found spare labour in the countryside by using the slack time in the agricultural year for industrial activities. This created rural employment which discouraged migration to the towns still further so that their industrial

58

functions and population shrank, creating a process of de-urbanisation. The beauty of this process is that it explains how towns could decline in a period of increasing prosperity and high wages, which ought to have guaranteed a good demand for urban goods and services.

The analogy cannot be simply applied to fifteenth century England, where the strength of foreign trade was a major difference; the biggest problem is whether the demand from the English country consumer was really strong enough to cause the effect seen in Japan. But it might fit better with the problems of 1520–60, when we could speculate that the upswing in the rural economy ran ahead of any improvement in the labour supply to towns, a situation which rapidly eased itself after 1560 as population growth filled the towns with people again.

So the key might lie in shortage of labour, which prevented towns from replacing their disease casualties and so made their goods too expensive through high wage costs, even if the workers could be found. We might assume that the bigger towns, where problems appear to be concentrated, were hit hardest by disease and so were worst affected by scarcity of labour. The theory does fit in well with observed complaints about the migration of textile manufacture to the countryside, and suggestions that towns were short of people. When applied to seventeenth century Europe, where there was undoubtedly both urban decline and rural industrialisation, the theory seems to work. But in later seventeenth century England, despite its stagnant population, we find not the urban troubles of the continent but a prosperity associated with increasing urbanisation. In any case, the connection between labour supply and the migration of industry is not at all clear, since English textile manufacture seems to have been forsaking some towns long before there was a problem of labour shortage, and conversely it can be shown to have flourished in some towns throughout the period in question. No advocate of urban decline has shown that any other industrial activity grew in the countryside to the detriment of the towns.

It does seem that the concept of a shortage of labour, with attendant high costs, could be the factor which lies behind at least part of the urban stresses we have been examining. It does provide a generalised force which can be applied irrespective of regional and individual circumstances to explain why the economies of many of the larger towns seem to have been under strain at certain times. But the fact that there is a theoretical explanation for the phenomenon of urban decline does not mean that it actually existed, or if it did, that the decline was as bad as has been suggested.

In conclusion, some general considerations deserve mention. There has always been an element of instability in towns, which by their very nature are liable to rapid growth in favourable circumstances and to stagnation or contraction when those circumstances alter: they can be seen as the barometers of economic change, rarely still for long. It will have become clear by this point that in the period with which this pamphlet deals there are ample examples of towns which grow, or are stable, or decline. There has never been a period in which this was not true. The challenge which faces us is that of separating the victims of this continuous, though usually low-level, process from that greater number of towns which would need to be failing if a crisis of general urban decline were to be identified.

The larger towns are prominent trouble spots, but this might be expected, for the big towns will by definition be those which have flourished in the circumstances of the immediate past, and as those circumstances change, so it is the larger towns that will be damaged. And the bigger the town, the greater the potential for decline, the more it has to lose. There is also the problem of separating the more specifically 'urban' phenomena from the more general ones. As we have seen above, both the mid-fifteenth and mid-sixteenth centuries were periods of general, national stress. Were the problems which towns suffered then peculiar to themselves or merely the local manifestations of a malaise which affected the whole country but which was mainly expressed and recorded in towns because of their political organisation and well-kept archives? We have also observed the striking changes which took place in the distribution of regional wealth over this period. When the towns of north-east England faltered, was this because they were towns or because they lay within that troubled region?

The student will be expecting some sort of answer to the question 'Did the towns decline?' It will have emerged from this pamphlet that no simple answer can be given, and the reader will

60

have been inclined in one direction or another by his or her response to the various problems of interpretation posed by the available evidence, with all its ambiguity. To a large extent the remaining uncertainties revolve around definitions and semantic questions. One's answer must depend on how the word 'town' is to be defined, and in particular how much weight is to be given to the experience of the larger towns, as against the more cheerful destiny of London and of the smaller towns. Again, the meaning of 'decline' has to be considered. We must specify the period concerned, and whether loss of population or of wealth or of function defines 'decline'. Should losses be absolute, or relative to other towns or to the countryside? If we are to speak of 'urban decline' what proportion of the total stock of towns must be affected, and does one measure this by counting individual towns or their accumulated populations? There are sufficient imponderables here to keep historians arguing about urban decline well into the future.

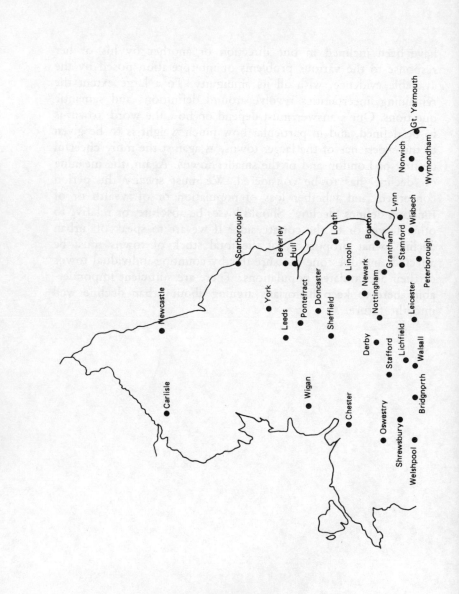

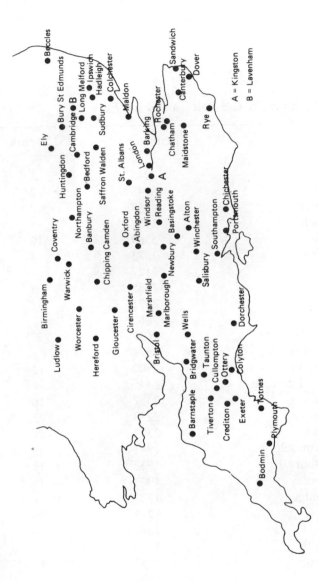

Map 3 *England and Wales, showing towns mentioned in the text.*

Appendix 1

The largest towns in the Poll Tax of 1377

Rank	Taxpayers	1520s rank
1. York	7248	5
2. Bristol	6345	2
3. Coventry	4817	7
4. Norwich	3952	1
5. Lincoln	3569	10
6. Salisbury	3373	4
7. Lynn	3127	–
8. Colchester	2955	8
9. Boston	2871	32
10. Beverley	2663	47
Newcastle	2647	(?7)
11. Canterbury	2574	6
12. Winchester	?2500	12
13. Bury St Edmunds	2445	9
14. Oxford	2357	16
15. Gloucester	2239	23
16. Leicester	2302	28
17. Gt. Yarmouth	1941	19
18. Shrewsbury	1932	15
19. Hereford	1903	11
20. Cambridge	1902	14
21. Ely	1772	39
22. Exeter	1696	3
23. Plymouth	1549	35
24. Worcester	1557	18
25. Hull	1557	33
26. Ipswich	1507	20
27. Northampton	1477	22

28. Nottingham	1447	41
29. Scarborough	1393	0
30. Stamford	1340	36
31. Newark	1178	0
32. Ludlow	1172	0
33. Southampton	1152	24
34. Pontefract	1085	0
35. Derby	1046	–
36. Lichfield	1024	30
37. Newbury	?1000	29
38. Huntingdon	984	27
39. Hadleigh	?917	34
40. Wells	901	–
41. Bridgnorth	?900	–
42. Bridgwater	888	–
43. Barking	?880	49
44. Chichester	869	38
45. Peterborough	850	–
46. Maidstone	844	21
47. Doncaster	800	0
48. Reading	?800	17
49. Cirencester	?746	–
50. Louth	684	–

Notes
0 = data unreliable or lost.
– = ranks below 50.
? = estimate.

Based on Hoskins [24], amended from various sources.
Newcastle omitted from ranking to conform with 1524–5, when it was not taxed.

Appendix 2

The largest provincial towns in the subsidy of 1524–5

Rank	Taxpayers	Rank in 1377
1. Norwich	1423	4
2. Bristol	1166	2
3. Exeter	1050	22
4. Salisbury	885	6
5. York	871	5
6. Canterbury	784	11
Newcastle	?	(11)
7. Coventry	725	3
8. Colchester	701	8
9. Bury St Edmunds	645	13
10. Lincoln	626	5
11. Hereford	611	19
12. Winchester	596	12
13. St Albans	*580	–
14. Cambridge	550	20
15. Shrewsbury	550	18
16. Oxford	542	14
17. Reading	531	48
18. Worcester	499	24
19. Gt Yarmouth	497	17
20. Ipswich	484	26
21. Maidstone	480	46
22. Northampton	477	27
23. Gloucester	466	15
24. Southampton	450	33
25. Rochester	*437	–
26. Crediton	*433	–

66

27. Huntingdon	433	38
28. Leicester	427	16
29. Newbury	414	37
30. Lichfield	391	36
31. Saffron Walden	*380	–
32. Boston	345	9
33. Hull	338	25
34. Hadleigh	311	39
35. Plymouth	310	23
36. Stamford	?308	30
37. Beccles	*307	–
38. Chichester	301	44
39. Ely	300	21
40. Taunton	*300	–
41. Nottingham	295	28
42. Tiverton	*289	–
43. Wymondham	*287	–
44. Bodmin	*285	–
45. Basingstoke	*274	–
46. Windsor	*267	–
47. Beverley	266	10
48. Alton	*260	–
49. Barking	256	43
50. Wisbech	*252	–

Notes
* = new since 1377.
? = estimate.

Based on various published sources, but primarily on material in J. Sheail, 'The regional distribution of wealth ... in the lay subsidy returns (1524–5)', (unpublished London Ph.D. thesis, 1968).

Appendix 3

The largest provincial towns in the Hearth Tax of 1662

	1520s
1. Newcastle	?
2. Norwich	1
3. York	5
4. Bristol	2
5. Exeter	3
6. Ipswich	20
7. Gt Yarmouth	19
8. Oxford	16
9. Cambridge	14
10. Canterbury	6
11. Worcester	18
12. Shrewsbury	15
13. Salisbury	4
14. Colchester	8
15. Hull	33
16. Coventry	7
17. Chester	?
18. Plymouth	35
19. Portsmouth	–
20. Lynn	–
21. Rochester	25
22. Lincoln	10
23. Dover	?
24. Nottingham	40
25. Gloucester	23
26. Bury St Edmunds	9
27. Winchester	12

28.	Sandwich	?
29.	Maidstone	21
30.	Leeds	–
31.	Leicester	28
32.	Northampton	22
33.	Chatham	–
34.	Ely	38
35.	Chichester	37
36.	Southampton	24
37.	Derby	–
38.	Ludlow	–
39.	Warwick	–

Notes
Ranking derived from total number of taxed hearths.
– = below 50 in 1520s ranking.
? = not taxed in 1520s.

Based on [24].

Appendix 4

Ranking of provincial towns by taxable wealth

1334	1524/5 1334 ranking in [ ]
1. Bristol ?£1900	1. [4] Norwich £749
2. York £1620	2. [1] Bristol £479
Newcastle £1333	3. [8] Coventry £448
3. Boston £1100	4. [26] Exeter £441
4. Norwich ?£1100	5. [10] Salisbury £411
5. Gt Yarmouth £1000	6. [9] Lynn £302
6. Oxford £914	7. [17] Ipswich £282
7. Lincoln ?£900	8. [13] Canterbury £269
8. Coventry £750+?	9. [2] York £230?
9. Lynn £770	10. [38] Reading £223
10. Salisbury £750	11. [49] Colchester £204
11. Shrewsbury ?£700	12. [24] Bury St Ed. £280
12. Winchester £625	13. [*] Lavenham £180
13. Canterbury £599	14. [34] Worcester £171
14. Hereford ?£550	15. [*] Maidstone £169
15. Southampton £511	16. [*] Totnes £144
16. Gloucester ?£510	17. [16] Gloucester £134
17. Ipswich ?£500	18. [5] Gt Yarmouth £125
18. Beverley £500	19. [14] Hereford £124
19. Cambridge ?£500	20. [7] Lincoln £124
20. Newbury £412	21. [20] Newbury £121
21. Plymouth £400	22. [3] Boston £111
22. Newark £390	23. [*] Hadleigh £109
23. Nottingham £371	24. [33] Hull £108
24. Bury St Ed. £360	25. [36] Leicester £107
25. Stamford £360	26. [6] Oxford £105
26. Exeter ?£350	27. [11] Shrewsbury £101

70

27. Northampton £350	28. [15] Southampton £101
28. Luton £349	29. [25] Stamford (£100)
29. Barking £341	30. [19] Cambridge £97
30. Scarborough £333	31. [46] St Albans (£95)
31. Ely £315	32. [*] Windsor £94
32. Derby £300	33. [27] Northampton £91
33. Hull ?£300	34. [*] Taunton £86
34. Worcester ?£300	35. [12] Winchester £86
35. Swaffham £300	36. [*] Marlborough £85
36. Leicester £294	38. [21] Plymouth £85
37. Grantham £293	38. [41] Huntingdon £82
38. Reading £293	39. [*] Ottery St Mary £79
39. Sudbury £281	40. [*] Dorchester £77
40. Peterborough (£275)	41. [*] Beccles £74
41. Huntingdon ?£270	42. [*] Crediton £74
42. Marshfield £270	43. [*] Maldon £72
43. Pontefract £270	44. [*] Basingstoke £67
44. Abingdon £269	45. [29] Barking £66
45. Banbury £267	46. [*] Long Melford £65
46. St Albans £265	47. [18] Beverley £63
47. Bridgwater £260	48. [*] Chichester £63
48. Doncaster £255	49. [*] Colyton £63
49. Colchester £250?	50. [*] Kingston on Thames £62
50. Leighton Buzzard £249	

Notes
1334 Assessed wealth.
   Data based on Glasscock [43].
   ? = amended figure based on material in Hadwin [43].
1524–5 Maximum sum paid in any one year.
   Data from Sheail (see Appendix 2).
   () = estimate.
   * = below 50 in 1334 rankings.

Appendix 5

The 57 largest provincial towns in 1377 and 1524–5
(Compiled from the top 50 in either ranking, assuming multipliers of 1.9 for 1377 and 6.5 for 1520s to convert taxpayers into population estimates.)

1. 22 towns with growing populations

	1377	1524–5	Change
Alton	1352	1690	+ 338
Basingstoke	1425	1781	+ 356
Beccles	1597	1996	+ 399
Bodmin	1482	1853	+ 371
Chichester	1651	1957	+ 306
Crediton	550	2815	+2265
Exeter	3222	6825	+3603
Hadleigh	1742	2022	+ 280
Huntingdon	1870	2815	+ 945
Lichfield	1946	2542	+ 596
Maidstone	1604	3120	+1516
Newbury	1900	2691	+ 791
Norwich	7509	9250	+1741
Reading	1520	3452	+1932
Rochester	1083	2841	+1758
Saffron Walden	1976	2470	+ 494
Southampton	2189	2925	+ 736
St Albans	2500	3770	+1270
Taunton	1024	1950	+ 926
Tiverton	1503	1879	+ 376
Windsor	1389	1736	+ 347
Wymondham	1493	1866	+ 373
	42,527	64,246	+21,719

2. 11 towns marginal between growth and contraction*

	1377	1524–5	Change
Barking	1672	1664	− 8
Bury St Edmunds	4646	4193	− 453
Cambridge	3614	3575	− 39
Canterbury	4891	5096	+ 205
Hereford	3616	3972	+ 356
Ipswich	2863	3146	+ 283
Northampton	2806	3101	+ 295
Salisbury	6409	5753	− 656
Shrewsbury	3671	3575	− 96
Wisbech	1638	1638	0
Worcester	2958	3244	+ 286
	38,784	38,957	+ 173

Notes
* = within a reasonable distance on either side of the multipliers applied to the tax data (1.8–2.0 for 1377, 6.0–7.0 for the 1520s) these towns give results indicating both growth and shrinkage. Towns in group 1 expand even when the highest figure for 1377 is compared with the lowest for 1377, and conversely for the contracting set in group 3.

3. 24 towns with declining populations

	1377	1524–5	Change
Beverley	5060	1729*	−3331
Boston	5455	2243	−3212
Bridgnorth	1710	715	− 995
Bridgwater	1630	1170	− 460
Bristol	12056	7579	−4477
Cirencester	1417	774	− 643
Colchester	5615	4557	−1058
Coventry	9152	4713	−4439
Derby	1987	1508*	− 479
Ely	3367	1950	−1417
Gloucester	4254	3029	−1225

Gt Yarmouth	3688	3231	− 457
Hull	2958	2197	− 761
Leicester	4374	2776	−1598
Lincoln	6781	4069	−2712
Louth	1300	982	− 318
Lynn	5941	1463	−4478
Nottingham	2749	1918*	− 831
Oxford	4478	3523	− 955
Plymouth	2943	2015	− 928
Stamford	2546	2002	− 544
Wells	1712	1437	− 275
Winchester	4750	3874	− 876
York	13771	5662*	−8109
	109,694	65,116	−44,578

Notes

* Northern town with possibility of under-assessment in 1520s. Beverley probably contained at least 4000 inhabitants in the 1550s.

Towns without adequate 1520s data: Carlisle, Doncaster, Ludlow, Newark, Newcastle, Pontefract, Scarborough.

Summary

1377	1524–5	loss
191,005	168,319	22,686

74

Select Bibliography

Books are published in London unless otherwise stated.

1. ECONOMIC AND SOCIAL BACKGROUND

(a) Medieval and General
[1] Baker, A. R. H., 'Changes in the later middle ages' in [5].
[2] Bean, J. M. W., 'Plague, population and economic decline in the later middle ages', *Economic History Review*, 15 (1962/3).
[3] Bolton, J. L., *The Medieval English Economy, 1150–1500* (1980). The best general introduction.
[4] Bridbury, A. R., *Medieval English Clothmaking: an Economic Survey* (1982). Lively, but partisan.
[5] Darby, H. C. (ed.), *A New Historical Geography of England* (Cambridge, 1973).
[6] Dyer, C., *Standards of Living in the later Middle Ages: Social Change in England c.1200–1500* (Cambridge, 1989). Which social groups gained from late medieval trends?
[7] McIntosh, M. K., 'Local change and community control in England 1465–1500', *Huntingdon Library Quarterly*, 49 (1986). Sees general expansion in the late fifteenth century.
[8] Miller, E., 'The fortunes of the English textile industry in the thirteenth century', *Economic History Review*, 22 (1965).

(b) Economic and Social Background: Early Modern
[9] Clay, C. G. A., *Economic Expansion & Social Change: England 1500–1700*, 2 vols (Cambridge, 1984). The best general survey.
[10] Palliser, D. M., *The Age Of Elizabeth: England under the later Tudors 1547–1603* (1983). Social and economic.

[11] Pound, J. F., *Poverty and Vagrancy in Tudor England* (2nd edn, 1986). The best short introduction.

(c) Economic and Social Background: Demography and Disease

[12] Goldberg, P. J. P., 'Female labour service and marriage in northern towns during the later middle ages', *Northern History*, 22 (1986). Impact of labour scarcity.

[13] Gottfried, R. S., *Epidemic Disease in Fifteenth Century England* (Leicester, 1978).

[14] Hatcher, J., 'Mortality in the fifteenth century: some new evidence', *Economic History Review*, 39 (1986).

[15] Hatcher, J., *Plague, Population and the English Economy 1348–1530* (1977). Excellent brief survey.

[16] Poos, L. R., 'The rural population of Essex in the later middle ages', *Economic History Review*, 38 (1985). Uses tithing rolls to show static population.

[17] Rutledge, E., 'Immigration and population growth in early fourteenth-century Norwich: evidence from the tithing roll', *Urban History Yearbook* (1988).

[18] Slack, P., *The Impact of Plague in Tudor and Stuart England* (1985).

2. GENERAL WORKS ON URBAN HISTORY AND URBANISATION

[19] Clark, P. and Slack, P., *Crisis and Order in English Towns 1500–1700* (1972). The introduction is an alternative to [20] as an exposition of this standard pessimistic view.

[20] Clark, P. and Slack, P., *English Towns in Transition 1500–1700* (1976).

[21] Corfield, P., 'Urban development in England and Wales in the sixteenth and seventeenth centuries' in *Trade, Government and Economy in Pre-Industrial England*, ed. Coleman D. C. and John, A. H. (1976). Urban populations.

[22] De Vries, J., *European Urbanization 1500–1800* (1984).

[23] Hohenberg, P. M. and Lees, L. H., *The Making of Urban Europe 1000–1950* (Cambridge, Mass., 1985).

[24] Hoskins, W. G., *Local History in England* (1959 and later edns). The rankings of provincial towns appear at pp. 174–8.

[25] Reynolds, S., *An Introduction to the History of English Medieval Towns* (Oxford, 1977). General survey.

[26] Thomson, J. A. F. (ed.), *Towns and Townspeople in the Fifteenth Century* (Gloucester, 1988). Essay collection.

[27] Tittler, R., 'The end of the middle ages in the English country town', *Sixteenth Century Journal*, 18 (1987).

3. THE DEBATE ON DECLINE

(a) Major Surveys (in order of publication)

[28] Bridbury, A. R., *Economic Growth: England in the Later Middle Ages* (1962; 2nd edn 1975). Lively and controversial optimist case.

[29] Dobson, R. B., 'Urban decline in late medieval England', *Transactions of the Royal Historical Society*, 27 (1977). The best brief survey of the pessimist case.

[30] Phythian-Adams, C. V., 'Urban decay in late medieval England' in Abrams, P. and Wrigley, E. A. (eds), *Towns in Societies* (Cambridge, 1978). Vigorous exposition of the pessimist case, perhaps over-influenced by the example of Coventry.

[31] Dyer, A. D., 'Growth and decay in English towns 1500–1700', *Urban History Yearbook* (1979). Perhaps more anti-pessimist than the author would now support.

[32] Phythian-Adams, C., 'Dr Dyer's urban undulations', *Urban History Yearbook* (1979). Reply to attack in [31].

[33] Bridbury, A. R., 'English provincial towns in the later middle ages', *Economic History Review*, 34 (1981). General restatement of optimist case.

[34] Goose, N. R., 'In search of the urban variable: towns and the English economy 1500–1650', *Economic History Review*, 39 (1986). Optimist attack on [19; 20].

[35] Reed, M. (ed.), *English Towns in Decline 1350–1800*, Leicester University Centre for Urban History (1986). Essay collection, contains [57] and [75] and others.

[36] Palliser, D. M., 'Urban decay revisited', in [26]. General survey of the controversy.

(b) Technical Issues

[37] Dobson, R. B., 'Admissions to the freedom of the City of York in the later middle ages', *Economic History Review*, 26 (1973). Unreliability of these figures.

[38] Kermode, J. I., 'Urban decline? The flight from office in later medieval York', *Economic History Review*, 35 (1982).

[39] Reynolds, S., 'Decline and decay in late medieval towns: a look at some of the concepts and arguments', *Urban History Yearbook*, (1980).

[40] Rigby, S. H., 'Urban decline in the later middle ages: the reliability of the non-statistical evidence', *Urban History Yearbook* (1984).

[41] Rigby, S. H., 'Sore decay and fair dwellings: Boston and urban decline in the later middle ages', *Midland History*, 10 (1985).

(c) Taxation Evidence

[42] Altreed, L. C., 'The King's interest: York's fee farm & the central government 1482–92', *Northern History*, 17 (1981).

[43] Glasscock, R. E. (ed.), *The Lay Subsidy of 1334* (1975). The basic statistics.

[44] Hadwin, J. F., 'The medieval lay subsidies and economic history', *Economic History Review*, 36 (1983).

[45] Hadwin, J. F., 'From dissonance to harmony in the late medieval town?' *Economic History Review*, 39 (1986). Tries to reconcile [46].

[46] Rigby, S. H., 'Late medieval urban prosperity: the evidence of the lay subsidies' *Reply by Bridbury, *Economic History Review*, 39 (1986). See also [45].

[47] Rigby, S. H., 'Urban decline in the later middle ages: some problems in interpreting the statistical data', *Urban History Yearbook* (1979).

[48] Tittler, R., 'Late medieval urban prosperity', *Bridbury rejoinder, *Economic History Review*, 37 (1984).

4. ARCHAEOLOGICAL EVIDENCE

[49] Astill, G. G., 'Archaeology and the smaller medieval town', *Urban History Yearbook* (1985).

[50] Hall, R. A. *et al.*, *Medieval Tenements in Aldwark, and other sites* (*The Archaeology of York*, Vol. 10:2, 1988).

5. BUILDINGS AND RENT

[51] Butcher, A. F., 'Rent and the urban economy: Oxford and Canterbury in the later middle ages', *Southern History*, 1 (1979).

[52] Butcher, A. F., 'Rent, population and economic change in late-medieval Newcastle', *Northern History*, 14 (1978).

[53] Elton, G. R., *Reform and Renewal: Thomas Cromwell and the Commonweal* (1973). The genesis of the Rebuilding Acts.

[54] Horrox, R. (ed.), *Selected Rentals and Accounts of Medieval Hull 1293–1528*, Yorkshire Archaeological Society Record Series, 141 (1983).

[55] Langton, J., 'Late medieval Gloucester: some data from a rental of 1455', *Transactions of the Institute of British Geographers*, 2:3 (1977).

6. MARKETS

[56] Britnell, R. H., 'The proliferation of markets in England, 1200–1349', *Economic History Review*, 34 (1981).

[57] Reed, M., 'Decline and recovery in a provincial urban network: Buckinghamshire towns, 1350–1800', in [35].

7. FOREIGN TRADE

[58] Carus-Wilson, E. M., *Medieval Merchant Venturers; Collected Studies* (Oxford, 1954).

[59] Carus-Wilson, E. M. and Coleman, O., *England's Export Trade 1275–1547* (1963).

[60] Childs, W. R. (ed.), *The Customs Accounts of Hull 1453–1490*, Yorkshire Archaeological Society, 144 (1984).

[61] Kermode, J. I., 'Merchants, overseas trade, and urban decline: York, Beverley and Hull c. 1380–1500', *Northern History*, 23 (1987).

[62] Pelham, R. A. (and Williams, D. T.), 'Medieval foreign trade: eastern ports' (and .. western ports), in Darby, H. C. (ed.), *An Historical Geography of England before AD 1800* (Cambridge, 1936).

[63] Power, E. E. and Postan, M. M., *Studies in English Trade in the Fifteenth Century* (1933).

[64] Ruddock, A. A., *Italian Merchants and Shipping in Southampton 1270–1600* (Southampton, 1951).

[65] Scammel, G. V., 'English merchant shipping at the end of the middle ages: some east coast evidence', *Economic History Review*, 13 (1960).

8. REGIONAL CHANGE

[66] Blanchard, I. S. W., 'Commercial crisis and change: trade and the industrial economy of the North-East 1509–1532', *Northern History*, 8 (1973).

[67] Hatcher, J., 'A diversified economy: later medieval Cornwall', *Economic History Review*, 22 (1969).

[68] Platts, G., *Land and People in Medieval Lincolnshire* (Lincoln, 1985).

[69] Schofield, R. S., 'The geographical distribution of wealth in England 1334–1649', *Economic History Review*, 18 (1965).

9. MISCELLANEOUS

[70] Horrox, R., 'Urban patronage and patrons in the fifteenth century', in Griffiths, R. A., *Patronage, the Crown and the Provinces in later Medieval England* (Gloucester, 1981). Political motives behind tax remissions.

[71] Starkey, T., *A Dialogue between Pole and Lupsett*, ed. Mayer, T. F. (Camden Society Fourth Series, 37) (1989).

10. INDIVIDUAL TOWNS

Towns are arranged in alphabetical order, after [72].

[72] *Victoria County History*: Gloucester (Gloucestershire, 4, 1988); Hull (Yorkshire East Riding, 1, 1969); Leicester (Leicestershire, 4, 1958); Oxford (Oxfordshire, 4, 1979); York (Yorkshire, 1961).

[73] Gottfried, R. S., *Bury St Edmunds and the Urban Crisis 1290–1539* (Princeton, NJ, 1982).

[74] Britnell, R. H., *Growth and Decline in Colchester, 1300–1525* (1986). An important work.

80

[75] Hutton, M., 'The urban craft group within the late medieval economy: the example of the Coventry weavers', in [35]. Does not entirely accept [76].

[76] Phythian-Adams, C. V., *Desolation of a City: Coventry and the Urban Crisis of the Late Middle Ages* (Cambridge, 1979). A classic study, but an over-stated case?

[77] Wilson, K. P., 'The port of Chester in the fifteenth century', *Transactions of the Historical Society of Lancashire and Cheshire*, 188 (1965).

[78] Carus-Wilson, E. M., *The Expansion of Exeter at the Close of the Middle Ages* (Exeter, 1963).

[79] Youings, J., *Early Tudor Exeter* (Exeter, 1974).

[80] Holt, R., 'Gloucester in the century after the Black Death', *Transactions of the Bristol and Gloucestershire Archaeological Society*, 103 (1985).

[81] Saul, A. R., 'English towns in the later middle ages: the case of Great Yarmouth', *Journal of Medieval History*, 8 (1982).

[82] Hill, J. W. F., *Medieval Lincoln* (Cambridge, 1948). Dated.

[83] Beier, A. L. and Finlay, R. (eds), *London 1500–1700: the Making of the Metropolis* (1986).

[84] Keene, D. J., *Cheapside before the Great Fire* (1985).

[85] Keene, D. J. and Harding, V., *Cheapside and the Development of London before the Great Fire* (forthcoming).

[86] Power, M. J., 'A "crisis" reconsidered: social and demographic dislocation in London in the 1590s', *London Journal*, 12 (1986).

[87] Rappaport, S., *Worlds within Worlds: the Structures of Life in Sixteenth Century London* (Cambridge, 1989). An optimist view.

[88] Rosser, G., *Medieval Westminster 1200–1540* (Oxford, 1989).

[89] Pound, J., *Tudor and Stuart Norwich* (Chichester, 1988).

[90] Goose, N. R., 'Decay and regeneration in seventeenth century Reading', *Southern History*, 6 (1984).

[91] Mayhew, G., *Tudor Rye* (Falmer, Sussex, 1987).

[92] Heath, P., 'North sea fishing in the fifteenth century: the Scarborough fleet', *Northern History*, 3 (1968).

[93] Champion, W. A., 'The Shrewsbury lay subsidy of 1525', *Transactions of the Shropshire Archaeological Society*, 64

(1985). Much of Mr Champion's fine work on Shrewsbury, used in the text, remains regrettably unprinted.

[94] Coleman, O., 'Trade and prosperity in the fifteenth century: some aspects of the trade of Southampton', *Economic History Review*, 16 (1963/4).

[95] Platt, C., *Medieval Southampton* (1973).

[96] Adey, K. R., 'Seventeenth century Stafford: a county town in decline', *Midland History*, 2 (1974).

[97] Dyer, A. D., *The City of Worcester in the Sixteenth Century* (Leicester, 1973).

[98] Keene, D. J., *Survey of Medieval Winchester*, II (Oxford, 1985). The best detailed account of an indisputably decaying city.

[99] Palliser, D. M., *Tudor York* (Oxford, 1979).

[100] Palliser, D. M., 'A crisis in English towns? The case of York 1460–1640', *Northern History*, 14 (1978).

Index

Abingdon, 71
Agriculture, 14–17, 21, 27, 51
Alton, 67, 72
Antwerp, 26, 51
Archaeology, 45

Banbury, 71
Barking, 34, 65, 67, 71, 73
Barnstaple, 34
Basingstoke, 67, 71–2
Beccles, 67, 71–2
Bedfordshire, 21, 40
Beverley, 20–1, 23, 40, 42, 64, 67, 70, 73–4
Birmingham, 57
Bodmin, 67, 72
Boston, 20–1, 23, 26, 40, 42, 64, 67, 70, 73
Bridbury, A., 12, 37
Bridgnorth, 65, 73
Bridgwater, 42, 65, 71, 73
Bristol, 26, 30, 40, 42, 54, 64, 66, 68, 70, 73
Bury St Edmunds, 34, 45, 55, 64, 66, 68, 70, 73

Cambridge, 54, 64, 66, 68, 70–1, 73
Cambridgshire, 21, 40
Canterbury, 34, 46, 55, 64, 66, 68, 70, 73
Capping, 29, 31
Carlisle, 74
Ceremonial, 49–50
Chatham, 52, 54, 69
Cheapside, 45–6
Chester, 30, 54, 68

Chichester, 34, 65, 67, 69, 71–2
Chipping Camden, 42
Cirencester, 65, 73
Clark, P. & Slack, P., 13, 52–4
Cloth, 15, 20–1, 23–8, 30–1, 34, 51–2, 55–6, 59
Colchester, 13, 31, 52, 55, 64, 66, 68, 70–1, 73
Colyton, 71
Cornwall, 40
Coventry, 10, 13, 28–9, 35, 40, 43–4, 64, 66, 68, 70, 73
Crediton, 66, 71–2
Cullompton, 43

Derby, 42, 54, 65, 69, 71, 73
Derbyshire, 21
Devon, 21, 34, 40
Disease, 13–14, 17, 25, 28, 53–4, 56, 59
Dobson, R., 13
Doncaster, 65, 71, 74
Dorchester, 71
Dorset, 40
Dover, 68

Ely, 42, 64, 67, 69, 71, 73
Epidemic, see under Disease
Essex, 20
Exeter, 26–7, 30, 34, 42, 44, 52, 54, 64, 66, 68, 70, 72

Fee farm, 47–8
Fishing, 23
Fulling mill, 21

83

Glasscock, R., 71
Gloucester, 31, 33, 46–8, 55, 64, 66, 68, 70, 73
Grantham, 71

Hadleigh, 34, 65, 67, 70, 72
Hadwin, J., 38, 71
Hales, J., 35
Hampshire, 20
Hereford, 30, 34, 64, 66, 70, 73
Hertfordshire, 20
Hoskins, W., 37
Housing, 42–7
Hull, 21, 26, 42, 46, 54–5, 64, 67–8, 70–1, 74
Huntingdon, 34, 42, 65, 67, 71–2

Ipswich, 34, 44, 64, 66, 68, 70, 73

Japan, 58–9

Kent, 20
Kingston on Thames, 71

Labour supply, 17, 51, 53, 56, 58–60
Lancashire, 57
Lavenham, 34, 42, 70
Leeds, 54, 69
Leicester, 20–1, 42, 48–9, 64, 67, 69–71, 74
Leighton Buzzard, 71
Leland, J., 47
Lichfield, 34, 42, 65, 67, 72
Lincoln, 12, 20–1, 23–4, 35, 40, 42, 47, 64, 66, 68, 70, 74
Lincolnshire, 16, 21, 25, 42
London, 15–16, 21, 24, 26, 28, 30, 32–4, 39–40, 45–6, 49, 51–4, 61
Long Melford, 42, 71
Louth, 65, 74
Ludlow, 65, 69, 74
Luton, 71
Lynn, Kings, 20–1, 23, 26, 40, 42, 54, 64, 68, 70, 74

Maidstone, 34, 65–6, 69–70, 72
Maldon, 71
Manchester, 57

Markets, 18
Marlborough, 71
Marler, R., 43
Marshfield, 71
Migration, 17, 58–9

Newark, 21, 65, 70, 74
Newbury, 34, 52, 55, 65, 67, 70, 72
Newcastle on Tyne, 20, 34, 54–5, 64, 66, 68, 70, 74
Norfolk, 21, 40
Northampton, 20, 34, 56, 64, 66, 69, 71, 73
Norwich, 13, 34, 43–5, 52, 54–5, 64, 66, 68, 70, 72
Nottingham, 21, 42, 54, 65, 67–8, 70, 74
Nottinghamshire, 21

Oswestry, 29
Ottery St Mary, 71
Oxford, 12, 20, 32, 46, 54, 56, 64, 66, 68, 70, 74
Oxfordshire, 40

Parliament, 43–4
Peterborough, 65, 71
Phythian-Adams, C., 13
Plague, see under Disease
Plymouth, 42, 55, 64, 67–8, 70–1, 74
Pontefract, 65, 71, 74
Population, 13, 14, 51
Portsmouth, 52, 54, 68
Prices, 14, 51

Reading, 34, 52, 55, 65–6, 70–2
Rebuilding Acts, 43–5
Rents, 45–7
Richard III, 47–8
Rigby, S., 38
Rochester, 34, 66, 68, 72
Rutland, 21

Saffron Walden, 67, 72
St Albans, 55, 66, 71–2
Salisbury, 21, 24, 34, 55, 64, 66, 68, 70 ,73
Sandwich, 69

84

Scarborough, 23, 42, 65, 71, 74
Sheffield, 57
Shrewsbury, 29, 47, 54, 64, 66, 68, 70, 73
Somerset, 20, 40
Southampton, 26, 32–3, 65–6, 69–72
Stafford, 56
Stamford, 20–1, 42, 65, 67, 70–1, 74
Starkey, 35
Sudbury, 71
Suffolk, 20
Swaffham, 71

Taunton, 34, 42, 44, 55, 67, 71–2
Tiverton, 34, 43, 67, 72
Totnes, 70
Trade, foreign, 15–16, 23, 25–7, 30–1, 51–2

Wages, 14, 16, 51
Wales, 25, 29, 31
Walsall, 56

Warfare, 25
Warwick, 69
Welshpool, 29
Westminster, 46
Wigan, 56
Wiltshire, 20, 40
Winchester, 12–13, 20, 24, 35, 45, 48, 64, 66, 68, 70–1, 74
Windsor, 67, 71–2
Wisbech, 34, 67, 73
Wool, 15, 20, 23, 27, 32
Worcester, 21, 34, 44, 64, 66, 68, 70–1, 73
Worcestershire, 35
Wymondham, 67, 72

Yarmouth, Great, 12, 23, 26, 42, 54, 64, 66, 68, 70, 74
York, 12, 17, 20, 24, 27, 35, 40, 42–3, 46, 48–9, 54, 64, 66, 68, 70, 74
Yorkshire, 16, 27